T0022034

SHOSTAKOVICH

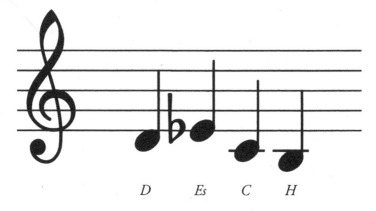

Dmitri Shostakovich's signature motif, which uses German notation to render an abbreviation of his name, D. S-ch.

SHOSTAKOVICH

A Coded Life in Music

BRIAN MORTON

First published in 2006 by
Haus Publishing Ltd
4 Cinnamon Row
London SW11 3TW

This first paperback edition published in 2021.

A CIP catalogue for this book is available from the British Library

The moral right of the author has been asserted

ISBN 978-1-913368-43-2
eISBN 978-1-913368-44-9

Typeset in Garamond by MacGuru Ltd

Printed in the UK by Clays Ltd, Elcograf S.p.A.

www.hauspublishing.com
@HausPublishing

To Jack

Contents

Introduction

On 29 August 1949, the Soviets detonated the RDS-1, the regime's first viable fusion bomb, a project that had occupied Soviet scientists in urgent secrecy since 1943. It changed the complexion of the Cold War in a moment. The Russians, those who were in the know at least, called the weapon Pervaya Molniya ('first lightning'). In the American inner circle, it was known as Joe-1.

Four months earlier, a small group of Russian intellectuals, including the head of the Union of Soviet Writers A. A. Fadeyev and the forty-two-year-old composer Dmitri Dmitriyevich Shostakovich, joined a motley crowd of left- and liberal-leaning Americans for the Cultural and Scientific Conference for World Peace at the Waldorf Astoria hotel in New York. They were, as Soviets abroad always were, accompanied by a protective gaggle of KGB men. Protesters of the right regarded the mere appearance of these men in New York as a Trojan horse, an ideological infiltration. The Reds weren't simply *under* the beds, in the common parlance; they were between the Waldorf Astoria's fine sheets. Much of the American intelligentsia had 'gone Red' in the 1930s. In 1906, in a book called *Warum gibt es in den Vereinigten Staaten keinen Sozialismus?*, a title often mistranslated minus the question mark as 'Why there is no socialism in the United States', the economist Werner Sombart had argued that almost any form of collectivism was alien to the 'American way'. In 1949, despite an uneasy wartime alliance with the Russians and some acceptance of the 'Uncle Joe' after whom the Russian bomb was nicknamed, a great swathe of Americans still agreed with him. The protesters outside the Waldorf Astoria came from the orthodox right, the Roosevelt-haters brought to life in Gore Vidal's novel *Washington, D.C.,* members of the Catholic Church, and those of other faiths who considered Communism to be blasphemous if not outright evil. Had they waited, or looked harder, they might not have thought their enemy quite so impressive or fearsome. The Cultural and Scientific Conference for World Peace was the moment when the American intelligentsia flip-flopped from fashionable socialism – and America, pace Sombart, had been a socialist country all through Franklin D. Roosevelt's New Deal – into paranoid anti-Communism, stage-managed and funded by the CIA and its still-progressive-sounding front, the Congress for Cultural Freedom. In the spring of 1949, the Russians made the job much easier.

At a panel session of the conference, Nicolas Nabokov, a Russian-born composer who had taken American citizenship ten years earlier, rose to his feet to pose a question he had taken some trouble to load. Nabokov had prepared chapter and verse. In a recent issue of *Pravda* – the official mouth-piece of the Soviet regime – the composers Igor Stravinsky, Arnold Schoenberg, and Paul Hindemith (of the three, only the last has the faded aura of a period piece; the others are still considered among *the* major moderns) had been denounced as 'lackeys of imperialist capitalism', their music 'obscurantist' and infected with 'decadent bourgeois formalism'. Stravinksy, who was in the process of becoming a superstar in America, was Nabokov's close friend. *Pravda*'s rhetoric was a shibboleth, its terminology familiar to anyone who had been exposed to Marxist criticism of the arts. Did Shostakovich, here in the US as a representative of the Soviet regime, support this position? Nabokov wanted to know.

The Russian heavies who were there to support Shostakovich – which meant in practice to watch for any sign of deviancy on their man's part – immediately cried foul. Shouting 'Provokatsiya!' ('provocation') and banging on tables in a style that would soon be made internationally famous by Joseph Stalin's successor, Nikita Khrushchev, they tried to shout down the question, but without much conviction, because they knew their man would come through. The scene was witnessed by the playwright Arthur Miller, who would later give definitive dramatic form to self-abasement in *The Crucible*. Shostakovich was handed a microphone and came to his feet like a marionette, his expression contorted by the tics and grimaces that had begun to afflict him in middle age. He barely raised his head but muttered miserably, 'I fully agree with the statement made in *Pravda*.'

There was shocked uproar when this was translated. Shostakovich had breached the solidarity that was supposed to apply among creative artists. He had implicitly attacked two great musicians, Schoenberg and Stravinsky, who had taken up residence in the United States. Years later, Shostakovich was to recall the occasion in his controversial memoir, *Testimony*, which may have been a sincere account of his life and opinions or may have been another kind of plant. In it, though, he is quoted as having said that he felt like a 'dead man' at the Waldorf Astoria. He knew that even endorsing the Soviet line did not guarantee his safety when he returned to the Soviet Union. Mere contact with the bourgeois world – even in a prisoner of war camp – could lead to liquidation. Shostakovich's smile was that of a condemned man. His appearance in New York was 'proof of life' as well as a rote endorsement of the Soviet cultural line. It did not guarantee him life or a living when he returned to the Soviet Union. He had already fallen foul of *Pravda* in its famous volte-face about his treasured opera *Lady Macbeth of Mtsensk*, which initially found favour and then was found to be, by Stalin himself in some accounts, full of ideological errors and lapses of tone.

Not many of those who came across Shostakovich in the spring of 1949 or in subsequent years remember him smiling, except with the rictus of a man in the dock. There are two significant photographs, taken some years apart. Both show a squat, bespectacled man whom one immediately and instinctively characterises as guarded and intense. (Family testimony concurs that, in middle and later life, Shostakovich was an intensely anxious man, obsessed with neatness and given to compulsive behaviours like sending himself postcards to see if the postal system was running smoothly – or perhaps to discover whether his mail was being intercepted.) In both photographs, he is far from home, in places where a mere word and some agile tradecraft might have guaranteed him safe exile. Though both occasions were ostensibly peaceful and celebratory, one might suspect he was a prisoner. In a very real sense, he was.

In the later photograph, one might say that he is at least among friends and fellow artists – fellow socialists, too, if the public persona and role are to be believed. It was taken at the George Hotel, Edinburgh in August 1962 during the city's renowned annual arts festival. The men flanking him might as well be prison guards, for all the warmth in his expression, though perhaps the lack of a common language made for a certain awkwardness. The two men are, respectively, a poet and a fellow composer. Hugh MacDiarmid was a literary maverick, marked by apparent deep contradictions. His public name was also a mask, a pseudonym for Christopher Grieve, and his politics were a sometimes-muddled mixture of Communist internationalism and intense Scottish nationalism, with an admixture of Major C. H. Douglas's quasi-fascist social credit thrown in.

The other man is Ronald Stevenson, an adopted Scot born in the north of England – the musicologist Nicolas Slonimsky described him as 'Brythonic' – who had spent some time in South Africa, an experience that had sharpened his instinct for political justice. He had come to present the honoured guest with the score of a huge piano work, some say the longest single movement piece ever written for the instrument. Alluding to the way classical composers created tributes to a revered ancestor by using the letters B–A–C–H in German notation as a musical cell (that sequence is sounded B-flat–A–C–B-natural), Stevenson's piece is called *Passacaglia on DSCH*, using an abbreviation of Shostakovich's name as a tribute to him.

The earlier photograph was taken at the Waldorf Astoria in 1949. At the extreme left (no pun intended) is Fadeyev. Opposite him, in profile, is the British science fiction writer Olaf Stapledon, over whom towers the smiling Arthur Miller, already a celebrated playwright. Next to Fadeyev, light-suited and holding a cigarette, is the twenty-six-year-old Norman Mailer, whose shy averted gaze sits oddly with the arrogant smirk that plays across his lower features. Lionised though he might have been since the publication of his best-selling war novel *The Naked and the Dead*, and self-possessed though he undoubtedly was by temperament and recent success, he must have felt slightly overwhelmed to find himself standing alongside one of the hero-artists of the late war, the composer of a symphony that in 1942 had been broadcast to millions worldwide in the most difficult circumstances imaginable. The apotheosis of Shostakovich's Symphony No. 7 in C major, *To the City of Leningrad*, as a symbol of resistance to fascism is one of the great musical stories of the twentieth century. Fifteen years before the Waldorf Astoria meeting, an American concertgoers' association had voted Jean Sibelius's Symphony No. 2 the greatest musical work of all time, a judgement that might seem unlikely but that reflects the tendency to give recent successes priority over older work like that of Beethoven or Mozart. By 1949, with Sibelius already some years into the long silence that marked his final three decades, no one would have questioned that the greatest living symphonist – and a master of other forms as well – was Shostakovich.

Mailer's air of self-consciousness may have been exacer-bated by the knowledge that he was just about to launch a savage and uncompromising attack on the man who had des-patched Fadeyev and Shostakovich as Soviet representatives to the Cultural and Scientific Conference for World Peace, organised by the National Council of the Arts, Sciences and Professions. Mailer astonished not just the other guests but his wife and close friends in the audience by taking a strong anti-Stalinist – indeed, Trotskyite – position, suggesting with impressive prescience that not just the United States but also the Soviet Union was drifting towards state capitalism. 'I have come here as a Trojan horse,' he declared. Given that many saw the conference in precisely the same light, it may have been less than the revelation he intended. The US State Department had already denounced the event as a Cominform front and had helped to orchestrate the anti-Communist protest and picket outside the Waldorf Astoria on the night of the conference's gala dinner.

The guest speakers on that occasion were the Harvard University scientist Harlow Shapley and Shostakovich. The Perroquet Room was an entirely appropriate location for the composer's address, which had him parrot the standard Soviet line on the duty of artists to promote a realistic and optimistic view of national life – 'When abroad, I feel myself to be a rep-resentative of the great Soviet people and of the world cultural centre, Moscow' – and to resist the abstract formalism and blandly tragic cosmopolitanism of bourgeois art. He had no time for Western journalists, damning them as 'uneducated, obnoxious, and profoundly cynical', only looking for lucrative scoops and bent on forcing him to speak 'daringly', which of course could have meant signing his own death warrant. As reported in the *New York Times*, Shostakovich said, 'Here I must stress that Party criticism of formalism in Soviet music is a life-giving source of musical creativeness. It helps all of us to paralyse alien influences and completely devote our art to the people and the motherland'. Shostakovich had many times put his name and signature to words written for him by others. At least on this occasion he was not required to speak them aloud; the address was read by an interpreter. Whether he meant those scripted words or his notorious condemnation of Schoenberg, Stravinsky, and Hindemith is a question that goes to the heart of the Shostakovich enigma.

The wider context of his visit to America is revealing. A matter of weeks before he flew to America, Shostakovich had been an unperson, his work condemned and proscribed by Stalin's cultural commissar, Andrei Zhdanov. It is a measure of the black ironies and perversities of life under the Soviet regime that when Zhdanov died in August 1948, six months after the Glavrepertkom (state commission for repertoire) edict that effectively denied Shostakovich a living and free expression, Shostakovich was quoted in an obituary article praising 'dear Andrei Alexandrovich [Zhdanov]' as a 'man of wide education and extraordinary erudition' whose death was a 'grievous, bitter loss'. Did he dance a little in private? Was the concept of 'private' meaningful in the Soviet orbit? Behind the thick glasses, Shostakovich kept his own council and played just enough of the game to stay alive.

Six months after Zhdanov's death, Shostakovich received

a late-night telephone call from Stalin himself. Shostakovich had spent many a sleepless night over the previous decade and a half waiting for the midnight knock on the door that would signal his arrest and disappearance into the hungry maw of what became known as the Gulag, or would represent the sharp pre-echo of the pistol shot that would end his life in some darkened cellar room. The life of Vsevolod Meyerhold, Shostakovich's mentor and one-time employer, had ended this way in the pre-war purges. In the event, Stalin merely 'asked' him to attend the Cultural and Scientific Conference for World Peace and, seemingly surprised that Shostakovich's work was still banned, lifted the proscription. The great micro-manager often seemed to forget his own decisions, a useful model for the later behaviour of national leaders as varied as Donald Trump, Jair Bolsonaro, Alexander Lukashenko – and, some might even add, Boris Johnson.

Such haphazard perversity is part of our received image of Soviet Communism, but American official attitudes and public opinion were every bit as fickle, even if the about-turns weren't quite as rapid. On 24 March 1949, Shostakovich landed at New York's LaGuardia airport, where he was met by Mailer and America's most distinguished composer, Aaron Copland. The broadcast premiere of Shostakovich's Seventh Symphony, from Radio City Music Hall, had pre-viously made him an international hero. On the day after the premiere, 20 July 1942, he had appeared on the cover of *Time* magazine, wearing the helmet of a volunteer fireman. No American composer had been required to douse fascist flames. Now, seven years later, in a much-changed political climate – and possibly with the disillusionment of seeing a hero in the undernourished, unfashionably dressed flesh – the response was decidedly lukewarm. Far from heroic, Shostakovich seemed shabby, neurasthenic, hidden behind the spectacles he fiddled with constantly. In an issue published on the day the Soviet delegation flew home, *Time* magazine rounded on him sharply, and other commentators noted with disgust his passive endorsement of *Pravda*'s condemnation of fellow composers and compatriots as 'decadents' and 'lackeys' of the West.

If America had chilled to Shostakovich, he failed to warm to Americans. Recalling the visit, he railed at the triviality of American journalism and the excessively personal questions asked by American reporters. The wartime alliance had papered over a vast gulf of incomprehension between the two superpowers; it was clear to all that the friendship was pragmatic and had been forged in spite of huge political and cultural differences. In a year haunted by 'alien' sightings and UFO landings in an America that had resisted terrestrial invasion, there could hardly have been a more otherworldly and alien a visitor than Shostakovich.

Americans of the time could only have had the dimmest understanding of how Shostakovich and his fellow artists had lived, not just during a war that cost some twenty million Russian lives but under a regime that since 1917 had practised terror on an unprecedented scale, though the names of Genghis Khan and Tamburlaine were sometimes adduced. Visitors from the US had included the journalists John Reed, who wrote a highly sanguine account of the Bolshevik

Revolution, *Ten Days That Shook the World*, and was given a hero's burial in the Kremlin Wall Necropolis when he died of typhus in 1920, and Lincoln Steffens, who had gone to observe the Communist experiment and provided a highly serviceable and adaptable quote when he reported back, 'I have seen the future, and it works.' Though there were steady rumblings of anxiety, not least among Mailer's new Trotskyite friends and the staff of the Trotskyite *Partisan Review*, originally published under the auspices of the John Reed Clubs, it wasn't until the revelations of the Twentieth Congress of the Soviet Communist Party in 1956 and Khrushchev's 'secret' revelation of Stalin's 'cult of personality' that the true horrors of the Stalinist terror became widely known in the West. The brutal repression of the Hungarian uprising would cure many of the remaining Western victims of the revolutionary fervour that the writer Lionel Trilling had characterised as 'scarlet fever', an infantile disorder. But the Moscow show trials and rumours of genocidal repression in the Soviet hinterland, added to the emergence of a second nuclear monolith on the planet, persuaded the majority of Americans that Russia and the values for which she stood were a threat to the exportable American way of life. With the war over and Europe settling into a new kind of attritional conflict, Shostakovich came to America as the – apparently willing – mouthpiece of an enemy state and of a political system violently inimical to the American way.

But how willing was he? What went on 'behind those frightened, very intelligent eyes', as someone who met him rather later put it? Why was he frightened? Was it fright his eyes were showing, or a kind of defiance? And how did that formidable intelligence work under a regime where intelligence itself, let alone a critical intelligence, was feared and suppressed? Americans are popularly supposed to lack a sense of irony. For Russians of Shostakovich's generation, irony was a genetic inheritance – and not just simple irony, but layers of it, like an onion.

At the final session of the Waldorf Astoria conference, late in the evening, Shostakovich had sat down alone at the piano and played the second movement from his Symphony No. 5 in D minor to the assembled delegates. This was the work that had been published twelve years earlier, bearing the apparently self-denying recantation *Practical Creative Reply of a Soviet Musician to Just Criticism*. In the story of Shostakovich, much is appearance. Getting at the reality underneath – or at least to some solid ground from which to make an objective judgement – is much harder. As we will see in Chapter Four, it is difficult to tell whether the composer's 'apology' was sincere, enforced, a merely routine obeisance, a terrified reaction to a climate of terror, or simply part of the complex anthropology of Russian life under the Soviets, in which opposition had to be expressed in coded forms and abjection might sarcastically suggest its opposite; these are long-standing questions, to some degree unanswerable and to a further degree irrelevant, but they will not go away, and for good or ill the Fifth Symphony is still widely described as Shostakovich's attempt to make amends for perceived failings.

Little remarked, compared to the premiere of the Fifth Symphony and later that of the Seventh, that cameo performance in New York offers important symbolic pointers to what might be called 'the Shostakovich problem'. Here was a man far from home, sitting in the heart of the enemy's camp, in front of a polite audience but with hostile demonstrators outside, playing a nakedly stripped-down version of one of his most famous and complex works – and the scherzo movement at that. Shostakovich was all too aware how black the joke – which is what 'scherzo' means – actually was, and how painfully forced his expression. Much later, he said, 'Look at the way I'm smiling in the photographs ... I answered all the idiotic questions in a daze and thought, "When I get back, it's over for me."' It wasn't, though. One of the most remarkable aspects of the story is that, unlike a host of other 'dissident' or merely unsatisfactory writers, artists, and intellectuals, Shostakovich survived. Part of the reason has to lie in the abstract nature of music (though the Soviet aesthetic rejected that premise wholesale). What did a symphony 'mean', after all? Even with a programmatic title attached, it was still an arrangement of sounds, a geometry of orchestral sections. The classical symphonies often contained some programmatic content, but it was structure and the dynamism of parts that made them symphonies, even when dedicated to a liberator, a loved one, or one's native country.

Shostakovich outlived his and his country's tormentor by more than two decades. He held on to his secret political opinions through all that time and to the very end. If he was a dissident, he was the most subtle of dissidents. If he was a loyal Communist, his commitment bore a very strange expression. It has to be concluded that in Shostakovich's case, the familiar, almost clichéd caprices of state terror actually worked to spare him, though what protected him most was the very success, at home and abroad, of the Fifth and Seventh Symphonies. By 1949, even though still profoundly suspect and under sustained pressure to suppress all personal elements in his work, he was too important and too prominent to be disappeared.

Right across the range of Shostakovich studies, from perspectives of the left and of the right, critics and biographers have found themselves hamstrung by the questions of Shostakovich's exact political sympathies – loyal Communist, visceral anti-Communist, loyal Communist disillusioned by Stalinism – and the sincerity of his personal and aesthetic opinions. Even an admiring bystander, the rock musician Elvis Costello, a self-professed amateur student of Shostakovich's work, expressed disappointment that Shostakovich recently should have been 'so rubbery of will' and a 'stooge of the state'. It is one of this book's modest contentions that Shostakovich's apparent about-turns – and all is appearance in this story – camouflage a basic consistency of attitude and can only be understood, beat for beat, in the rapidly changing contexts of Soviet politics and cultural 'policy'. When art is politicised, the minutiae of cultural politics play as active a role as aesthetics. At some point, someone will write a study of Shostakovich from such a point of view, but even after three decades of 'openness' and 'reconstruction', such a task is closed to any but a Russian insider. Somewhat more aggressively, I suggest that Shostakovich's admittedly strange career is not sui generis in comparison to those careers of his Russian contemporaries and many other great artists. What of Beethoven's disillusioned rededication of the *Eroica* symphony? The comparison is tricky, but not absurd. Does it not suggest a change of heart, or at least the necessity of responding to political contingency? In a similar way, why, when dealing with the vexed – but now largely resolved – question of Shostakovich's autobiographical *Testimony* (to which we'll come shortly), do the same critics never mention Robert Craft's remarkable – some would say incredible – recall of Stravinsky's conversations and comments? Do we distrust his *Memories and Commentaries* and *Expositions and Developments* and reject Craft as a self-serving ventriloquist, the way we have distrusted *Testimony* and condemned its 'editor', Solomon Volkov, as a forger?

It is from Craft, Stravinsky's friend and amanuensis (some would say ghostwriter), that we have that vivid description of Shostakovich's frightened eyes. Craft had the opportunity to observe Shostakovich at close quarters during Stravinsky's much-feted 'all is forgiven' visit to Russia in 1962. Forgiveness only ran one way, though. While it suited the new Russia to welcome back a famous son, Stravinsky himself was disinclined to forget past slights and calumny, and by Shostakovich's own account offered one Communist party apparatchik the head of his walking stick to shake instead of his hand. Memoirs of the period are infamously contradictory. Events are remembered in one light by one participant and in quite another from the other side of the room, or the ideological fence. What Craft's account fails to mention is that, a dozen years earlier, Shostakovich himself had passively endorsed the Soviet condemnation of Stravinsky, despite his deep personal admiration of his fellow composer's work. It is clear, from *Testimony* and elsewhere, that words had been put into his mouth, that he was, in the popular parlance, toeing the party line. Though he distrusted Stravinsky's cosmopolitanism, he may have envied the man, not so much for his international reputation – Shostakovich was himself known throughout the West – but for the seeming ease of it. Where Shostakovich was admired for his courage, his toughness, the mixture of tragedy and satire in his work, Stravinsky was feted as a superstar, a man equally at ease in Paris, New York, or Los Angeles.

The two composers met twice in early October 1962. They flanked their hostess at a formal reception and were thrown together again a few days later at the banquet that marked the climax of Stravinsky's visit. It was here that Craft observed Shostakovich as being handsomer than expected and almost 'boyish-looking', but nervously gnawing at his fingers, chain-smoking, and looking poised (if that's the right word) between uncertainty and tears. At least in 1962, the composer could not have feared death on his return home, but the shadow of Stalin – dead almost ten years – and of Stalinism was no lighter and no less extensive. There had been, however, a major shift in Soviet cultural policy, not least in its attitude to 'problematic' artists like Shostakovich. The change was highly selective and dependent on an individual's willingness to make at least some token observance of the official line. Boris Pasternak had died unreconciled in 1960, having been awarded – and forced to decline – the Nobel Prize in Literature two years before. But the international success of *Doctor Zhivago* had created deep Western interest in Russian literature, especially that of a poetically adversarial nature, and to some degree Shostakovich, too, benefited from that fresh sympathetic attention. The charisma of the 'Leningrad symphony' had worn off with the end of the war and the inevitable transmutation of friends into Cold War enemies. Now, though, there was a thaw, however brief and partial.

Shostakovich may have been galled that a figure like Stravinsky could make a reputation and a significant fortune abroad – he was, after all, the first classical composer whose wider reputation had been secured largely through gramophone recordings – but, while Shostakovich did not enjoy the patronage of the broadcaster CBS, he must have been aware that his own international reputation was once again secure. The previous year, his Symphony No. 4 in C minor, a dark and disturbing work that contains some of the loudest orchestral music ever written, had at last been performed in the USSR. The premiere came almost thirty years after the work's completion, the original score having been deemed counter-revolutionary (read: the cultural commissars simply didn't understand it) and withdrawn in rehearsal. A matter of three months before Stravinksy's visit, with its celebratory concert series, Shostakovich himself had been the subject of that important retrospective in Edinburgh, at which his Fourth Symphony had been prominently featured.

So why, in the Edinburgh photograph with MacDiarmid and Stevenson, does his expression still seem so pessimistic and occluded? Perhaps because the first performance of his latest symphony, the Twelfth, had been greeted with great dismay, hailed as his worst major score, and damned for its lurid repetitions and crudities. Stevenson suggested that, during that visit to Scotland at least, Shostakovich seemed utterly, self-denyingly absorbed in his music and in its correct performance – faster, always faster. He resembled a 'lightning conductor', channelling immense forces while seemingly passive and almost craven himself. When the two composers met in Moscow six years later, on the Russian's home ground, there was a lighter side to their conversation: a shared interest in football and the respective merits of Glasgow Rangers and Dynamo Moscow.

There are other potential explanations for Shostakovich's diffidence. No Soviet citizen abroad could afford to relax even for a moment. Even the smallest sign of wavering revolutionary vigilance could be interpreted as complicity; the merest exposure to the bourgeois virus could result in infection. Communism and Western capitalism each regarded the other as a pandemic that could sweep through society if appropriate exclusions and rigorous isolation were not practised. While Shostakovich presumably no longer feared the midnight knock on the door – there was a running joke in pre-war Russia about the 'little suitcase' everyone kept packed and ready against that moment – he still lived under the strictest monitoring and was still able to generate enormous controversy. He had been elected as delegate to the Supreme Soviet of the USSR in May and was already first secretary of the Composers' Union, something that required him, at last, to join the Communist party, but even then Shostakovich was still subject to ferocious strictures. His Symphony No. 13 in

B-flat minor would be premiered in December to a storm of criticism he must have wearily anticipated. Eight days later, he attended the premiere in Leningrad of his opera *Katerina Ismailova*, a 'politically correct' revision of the 1932 work *Lady Macbeth of Mtsensk*, which, despite its popular success, had called down the wrath of Stalin. Somewhere in between, Shostakovich married his mistress, Irina Supinskaya – but there is no sign of happiness in that Edinburgh photograph, still less in the surviving newsreel footage, which proves that his expression isn't simply a stilted moment in an otherwise relaxed meeting. (Western editors liked to catch Russian visitors looking glum. It was a nicely graphic way of showing that dialectical materialism didn't bring happiness.)

The other factor that bore on Shostakovich was the same that had troubled him in 1949. He was, quite simply, ill at ease in the West and viscerally resistant to its ways. In the autumn of 1962, Britain was still buzzing in the aftermath of the Lady Chatterley trial, which had resulted in an openly available paperback edition of D. H. Lawrence's worst novel – which had previously circulated in various underground forms, much as dissenting literature did in the Soviet Union. How ironic all this must have seemed to a man who had been condemned for the 'pornographic' elements in his *Lady Macbeth of Mtsensk* and had witnessed the censorship of his work. Also, Shostakovich had just taken part in a festival that had seen the institution of a celebrated writers' congress, a forerunner of the Edinburgh International Book Festival. The following year, it became notorious when a young woman called Anna Kesselaar was wheeled round a balcony at the main venue (avoiding the iron hand of the Lord Chancellor, who forbade moving nudes but grudgingly allowed still tableaux; the organisers argued that Kesselaar was *being moved*, not moving herself, and was therefore immune to prosecution, a nicely Pharisaic or Soviet touch). The original congress, already concerned with a more anarchic and individualistic view of 'freedom' than the one promulgated in New York in 1949, had been organised by none other than Sonia Orwell, the widow of the man who had created the iconic fictional version of the superpower stand-off in *Nineteen Eighty-Four.* And if the chronological 1984 still seemed far distant, the reality of Shostakovich's world in 1962 was disturbingly close to George Orwell's dystopia. Thought crime and doublethink were the Russian's everyday realities, not aspects of some dystopian fantasy.

The Edinburgh visit offered a sharp instance of how doublethink worked in practice. The great cellist Mstislav Rostropovich, who was conducting some of his friend's work at the festival, recalls that at a press conference a reporter asked Shostakovich if he had agreed with the party's criticism of him in 1948. 'Yes, yes, yes,' said Shostakovich, 'and not only do I agree, I am *grateful* to the party.' It was a standard line, but the composer then turned to Rostropovich and said angrily, 'That son of a bitch! How could he dare ask that question? Doesn't he understand that I can't answer it?'

As if to prove how shallow – or utopian – all the talk of peace had been, mere weeks after Shostakovich's visit to Edinburgh, and only days after Stravinsky returned to the US, an American U-2 spy plane returned incontrovertible evidence of a Soviet military build-up, including medium-range nuclear missiles, on what President John F. Kennedy called the 'imprisoned island' of Cuba. The world was plunged into a crisis that threatened all-out atomic war. There were whispers of a power struggle in the Kremlin, a sharp reminder of the old days of ruthless factionalism. The Kennedy brothers wavered, listening to the advice of hawks and doves. American submarines and service ships slipped their moorings in a Scottish loch and put quietly out to sea. For nearly two weeks, the whole world lived with the seemingly imminent threat of destruction. Questions about political rightness or wrongness looked set to vanish in a mushroom-shaped cloud.

Few modern artists more completely represent the contradictions of the age – political, aesthetic, psychological – than Shostakovich. Inevitably, much politically inspired nonsense has been written about him, masking a sadder and still more remarkable reality. At the peace conference in 1949, someone else was able to observe him at close quarters. Where later Craft was an American visiting Russia, the composer Nicolas Nabokov was a Russian-born exile in the United States. He sat close alongside Shostakovich and witnessed the same nervous behaviour Craft had noted: twitching, shredding the filters of his cigarettes, symptoms of deep unease, and a sharp contrast to the stony-faced impassivity of the other Soviet delegates. 'To me,' wrote Nabokov in his memoir, *Bagázh*, 'he seemed like a trapped man, whose only wish was to be left alone, to the peace of his own art and to the tragic destiny to which he, like most of his countrymen, had been forced to resign himself.'

History will not leave Shostakovich alone in death any more than in life. Between his death in 1975 – when the second edition of Nabokov's memoir was published – and now, there has been a flood of biographical and critical writing, favourable, critical, revisionist, counter-revisionist, and even, in the hall of mirrors called postmodernism, counter-counter-revisionist. It has become customary to begin any new account of Shostakovich's life with some version of 'the Volkov affair' and some conclusion about the reliability or otherwise of *Testimony*. I have preferred to relegate such a discussion to my final chapter, where it belongs, and to use the memoir as a source when its narrative relevance seems unambiguous. I have not assumed that *Testimony* is the crux to any understanding of Shostakovich, his life, and his work. That seems to me wrong-headed in the circumstances, which are exceptional. Instead, I have tried to provide a straightforward narrative of the composer's life and the evolution of his music. Our instinctive critical paradigms suggest that these two courses should describe a relatively smooth trajectory: naivety gives way to mature wisdom, obscurity to recognition; 'influence' reverses polarity as the susceptibilities of youth are transcended and the artist begins to transmit his own language to subsequent generations. Death – with or without a prior disillusionment and decline – marks the end.

And yet, life and work – and, still more, life and times – are only awkwardly twinned in even the most tranquil of lives. More than most creative geniuses, Shostakovich refuses to fit the paradigm. His genius was highly precocious, his influences overcome with rare speed and confidence. His circumstances were so strange and extreme that his work was not allowed to evolve in an organic way and was not just acted on by his own and international society, but was acted on with bizarre capriciousness. If Shostakovich had grown up in Geneva – or in New York or Edinburgh – the course of his life would inevitably have been very different, but it would also have lacked the deep absorption in Russia and the profound commitment to the Russian people and their culture that gives the work its only recoverable consistency. Heard in sequence – whether the sequence of composition or of first performance – Shostakovich's oeuvre can seem confusingly haphazard. How could the composer of the great symphonies also have written the drumbeating *The Fearless Regiments Are On The Move*? Unless one is completely comfortable with MacDiarmid's proposition that genius is volcanic and throws out vast amounts of rubbish for only small amounts of real ore, the body of Shostakovich's work is peppered with slight and unworthy compositions that don't seem to belong to the composer of the great symphonies, the concertante works, and the beloved opera.

As with most such questions, the rhetorical element is not absolute. There is almost always an external reason that explains Shostakovich's apparent regressions. And it is worth saying that such moments can very easily be found in most creative lives. Did Shakespeare compromise his art to secure the approval of the 'regime'? It is thought that Elizabeth I recognised herself in Shakespeare's Richard II. Might Shakespeare have been 'cancelled' or disappeared as a result? Or was he able swiftly to mollify? We seem untroubled by such considerations, and we might argue that Shakespearean England is not Soviet Russia. But the parallel just about holds.

With Shostakovich, one is always looking for 'the figure in the carpet', for some pattern of political and/or psychological consistency that provides a steady course through the life and music. Unfortunately, no such single pattern presents itself convincingly. Recognising that, this book attempts to listen for the deeper pulse of the life and the music, not so much to transcend the unavoidable ironies, duplicities, and double games as to set them aside for a moment. Its conclusion is clear: history refuses to leave him alone not because of unpurged guilt or psychological opacity, but very simply because Dmitri Dmitriyevich Shostakovich stands among the very greatest exponents – and perhaps the last great exponent – of what we still uneasily call classical music.

One

On 14 September 1960, the recently appointed first secretary of the Composers' Union delivered an address to an open session. As so often, it was difficult to tell whether Dmitri Shostakovich's discomfort came from the words he was required to read or from sheer nervousness and embarrassment at being dragged into the spotlight, but there was no mistaking the animation with which he delivered one (possibly unscripted) line: 'For all that is good in me, I owe a debt to my parents.' Even in that period, it would probably have been circumspect to claim that one had been formed and nurtured in the warm embrace of Soviet Communism, suckled by Mother Russia, raised to adulthood by the rigours of dialectical materialism. But perhaps Shostakovich was speaking in code, or with the kind of implicit irony that hovers like smoke around most of his recorded statements. 'For all that is good in me... for all the rest – my ideological "errors" and shortcomings, my artistic "failures", this awkward wretch I have become – well, who can be blamed for that? Myself? You? The great Soviet state?' But the first secretary's head had gone back down, and he continued to read his text in the familiar monotone reserved for officially sanctioned statements.

It is a pity that a decade and a half later, as he signed the manuscript pages of his memoir *Testimony* for the book's editor, Solomon Volkov, the sixty-nine-year-old composer seemed to have so few memories of his mother and father, or of his childhood. It seems, though, that his comment to the Composers' Union was accurate. The Soviet state may have shaped his career, but its influence is unsurprisingly exaggerated in the familiar accounts. Whatever else in him was good or ill certainly seems to have come from his mother and father.

Dmitri Boleslavovich Shostakovich, the composer's father, worked as senior keeper in the St Petersburg Chamber (Palace) of Weights and Measures, which had been founded by Dmitri Mendeleev, deviser of the periodic table of elements. He had originally trained in histology, a branch of biology specialising in organic tissues, and it is not precisely clear what was his function at the Chamber of Weights and Measures. After Mendeleev's death, the institute was run down, and Dmitri Boleslavovich found work as manager at the Rennenkampf estates at Irinovka. He also worked in munitions during the First World War.

The family's political past was somewhat chequered, though by no means unusual for their class and time. The paternal line had been Polish. A Bolesław Szostakowicz had been involved in the January Uprising in the Russian Kingdom of Poland, an attempt to restore the Polish-Lithuanian Commonwealth. Weakened by defeat in the Crimean War, Russia had been vulnerable to internal dissent. Many, including those connected to the conspiracy only very tenuously and by association rather than strong conviction, were sent into exile following an unsuccessful assassination attempt on Tsar Alexander II.

Nine years later, in 1875, Dmitri Boleslavovich was born in Narym, Siberia, close to Tomsk, which was to become a closed city ('Atomsk') under the Soviet regime. Dmitri Boleslavovich Shostakovich came to St Petersburg to study, and there he met Sofiya Vasilievna Kokoulina, another former Siberian exile, whose family had become wealthy running the Lena mines in Eastern Siberia, the source of that almost mythical substance that haunted the Cold War: Russian gold.

The Americans who met the composer Shostakovich in 1949 and were dismayed, even disgusted, by his pasty, pock-marked face and neurasthenic manner may – the more generous ones – have put down his condition to the rigours of the late war in which he was known to have acted bravely in a civilian capacity but, like all citizens of St Petersburg, to have suffered considerable privation. In fact, the young Shostakovich was frequently ill – or, more accurately, never entirely well. He suffered lymphatic tuberculosis as a child and was operated on. During the Civil War of 1918 to 1920, when the allies blockaded the new Bolshevik regime, he suffered severe malnutrition and further bouts of tuberculosis. So serious was his situation that, while Shostakovich was studying at the Petrograd (now St Petersburg) Conservatory, the school's director, the composer Alexander Glazunov, applied on his behalf for extra rations, not so that a precocious young man could luxuriate in extra food but, quite simply, to ensure his survival. In addition, Shostakovich had suffered from a grumbling appendix, which he believed had denied him success in the International Chopin Piano Competition in 1927. He had an appendectomy later that year.

The grumbling of hunger probably had a greater impact, though.

There had been happier and more plentiful times – notably the summers spent at Irinovka (in photographs, 'Mitya' looks blissful standing between his sisters) – but even before the revolution, everyday life was spartan by Western standards, and there was always the additional fear of a visit by the Okhrana, the tsarist secret police, forerunners of the Cheka, OGPU, NKVD, and ultimately KGB of the Soviet years. The Shostakoviches had some reason to fear such a visit. Before considering the family's political background, it is worth noting that the first twelve years of Dmitri Dmitriyevich's life were precisely bracketed by the Russian revolutions: that of 1905, and then those of 1917. Less than two years before his son's birth, Dmitri Boleslavovich was present with his brother-in-law at the infamous Bloody Sunday massacre of 22 January 1905,* a turning point in Russian history in which tsarist troops fired on a crowd of people in Palace Square who were protesting about food shortages. His son must have grown up with stories of that terrible day, and was certainly old enough to have heard news of the Lena massacre, which had an even more immediate family resonance. Discontent in the goldfields had come to a head on 13 March 1912 when rotten meat was distributed to hungry families by one of the company-owned stores. Anyone who has seen the classic 1925 Sergei Eisenstein film *Battleship Potemkin* will have some sense of how this might have been received. Even

*This book uses Gregorian dates.

in black and white, the sight of maggots wriggling on meat rations sticks in the mind. The strike that followed engulfed most of the mines. The strike leaders were arrested in mid-April. On the following day, a crowd of 2,500 marched on the Nadezhdinsky goldfield to demand their release. In a tragic echo of Bloody Sunday, troops fired on the crowd; 270 were killed and a further 250 wounded.

There is no direct evidence of the impact this had on Sofiya Shostakovich, whose family had by all accounts been enlightened administrators, committed to improving the workers' conditions. Like her husband, she was a Narodnik, a supporter of the people's party, and both were passionately committed to democracy. Their beliefs were shared by other members of the family. Shostakovich's paternal grandfather had been an adherent of Zemlya i Volya ('Land and Will'), a revolutionary group much influenced by Nikolai Cherny-shevsky, the utopian socialist and author of the novel *What Is To Be Done?*, which had a strong impact on Vladimir Lenin (who borrowed the title). Several of Shostakovich's uncles and aunts had been active in anti-tsarist politics before the revolution of 1905. Like many of their class, his mother's sister Nadia, who lived with the family in St Petersburg, was radicalised by Bloody Sunday and became an early Bolshevik, a detail inevitably made much of in official Soviet hagiographies of the composer. The discovery of a founding spirit in the family tree was a little like discovering royal ancestry. Dissent was dangerous throughout Shostakovich's life; only the watchers changed. On at least one occasion, the family home on Ulitsa Podolskaya was raided by Okhrana agents searching for inflammatory literature. Mercifully, they found none. The fiancé of another aunt, Lyubochka, was arrested on a trumped-up charge of murdering a policeman and freed only with difficulty.

It is hard to exaggerate the impact of this background on the young composer-to-be. It is also important to clear away any illusion that there was a smooth continuum between the two Russian revolutions, that they were simply different aspects of the same process. The revolution of 1905 was populist and democratic, libertarian in its essence. That of 1917 was fiercely centralist and authoritarian, avant-gardist in spirit, and totalitarian to the core. All his life, Shostakovich sustained a passionate and unswerving commitment to the Russian people, their traditions, and their self-defining wisdom. It is against that conviction – not against his inconsistent and often puzzling reactions to the vagaries of Soviet Communism, and not against his attitude to Marxism–Leninism or the 'science' of dialectical materialism – that all his work has to be judged and understood.

Dmitri Dmitriyevich Shostakovich was born in St Petersburg on 25 September 1906. He was to have been called Jaroslav, but the priest overruled the parents on grounds that are not entirely clear – perhaps to preserve the continuity of the father's given name, though the patronymic Dmitriyevich would have taken care of that. There was an older sister, Maria, born three years before him; a second sister, Zoya, was born in 1908.

With his aunt Nadia also living in the house and his father much absent, it was women who largely defined Shostakovich

– not unusual for that time and class but profoundly important nonetheless. In later life, Shostakovich remained susceptible to female influence and retained a romantic and somewhat courtly view of the gender. The first tragedy of his life was the premature death of his much-loved aunt Lyubochka in 1914.

When we describe Shostakovich as a precocious talent, it shouldn't be taken to mean that, like some St Petersburg Mozart, he began writing piano pieces at the age of three or four, or that he had a true prodigy's instinct for performance, picking at the keys as soon as he could reach them. By some standards, Shostakovich was a relatively late starter. There is little doubt that his childhood home was full of music and that he began to learn piano before his teens. Dmitri Boleslavovich apparently liked to sing Gypsy songs to the accompaniment of his guitar. The conductor and author Nicolas Slonimsky, who often didn't let the facts get in the way of a good story, rather optimistically described Sofiya as 'a professional pianist'. She was, in fact, a teacher. Though conservatory trained, she is probably best considered an accomplished amateur, much in demand to play at the houses of friends and her husband's colleagues. At first, it was assumed that Dmitri would become an engineer like his father, a role that sat well with the Shosta-koviches' progressive and meliorist philosophy. Mother Russia needed skilled men.

Shostakovich's first formal musical experience that we know of was a family visit to the opera in 1914, when he was eight. They saw a production of *The Tale of Tsar Saltan*, which of course includes the famous test piece 'Flight of the Bumble-bee'. An avid reader, Shostakovich may well have known the story already; Alexander Pushkin was a favourite. Whatever he made later in life of Nikolai Rimsky-Korsakov's 'perfumed' music (the description is Neville Cardus's), which does seem the antithesis to his own, it is worth noting that Shostakovich's Op. 1, a scherzo written when he was thirteen, is a homage to Rimsky-Korsakov. Not much perfume surrounded Shostakovich's mature music, though occasionally the scent of sulphur could be detected. Rimsky-Korsakov revised the works of Modest Mussorgsky – whom the young Shostakovich revered for his encapsulation of the soul and spirit of old Russia – after the latter's death; Cardus likened this intervention to letting Algernon Charles Swinburne loose on the works of Robert Burns.

Not until the following year, when the war in the East had settled to its own brutal stalemate, did Sofiya persuade Shostakovich to sit at the piano and practise some simple scales. What followed does perhaps merit terms like 'precocity' or even 'genius', at least as told by the proud family. He seemed to have the ability to reproduce any music played to him, often pretending to read a score while actually playing from memory. The boy seemed to absorb music like oxygen. His progress was disconcertingly rapid. Bored with academic exercises, he quickly outgrew his first teacher, Ignati Gliasser, and outdistanced his classmates. Private lessons with Alexandra Rozanova were more fruitful. By the age of ten, he had acquired a considerable repertoire. He mastered Johann Sebastian Bach's *The Well-Tempered Clavier* in its entirety and, according to the author David Fanning, was playing Ludwig van Beethoven's *Hammerklavier* sonata by the age of fifteen.

Early Beethoven studies continued to surface in his work. The rondo 'Rage Over a Lost Penny' is referenced in Shostakovich's Piano Concerto No. 1 – a pastiche, but a respectful one, for all the uproar.

All Shostakovich's diffidence and awkwardness disappeared when at the piano. Someone who saw him perform at a family friend's house commented, 'The skinny boy is transformed into a bold musician with a man's strength and captivating rhythmic drive.' There was another important development, which saw the slow evolution of the B–A–C–H motif into D–S–C–H, a private musical signature that remains enigmatic and occluded but unmistakable once it has been fully met. Dull as Gliasser's teaching may have been, it did not extinguish the creative spark. Shostakovich's first known composition has not survived, and there is no reason to think that *The Soldier (Ode to Liberty)*, a piano piece, was anything other than a rather conventional expression of wartime sentiment, but it was a sign of things to come (and cheerfully gives the lie to any suggestion that Shostakovich only ever wrote patriotic works at the command of his Soviet masters).

Sometime in 1917, he also wrote *Funeral March for the Victims of the Revolution*. The piece was subsequently destroyed, but its main theme was to be a revenant, hauntingly repeated in the opening movement of his Symphony No. 2 and heard once again thirty-five years later in the closing movement of his Symphony No. 12. What dents the seeming orthodoxy of their respective subtitles, *To October* and *The Year 1917*, is the knowledge that the original piece was inspired by the sight, when Shostakovich was ten, of a young boy hacked to death by a Cossack on the Letny Prospekt, apparently for stealing an apple. There may have been little continuity between the ideals of 1905 and the brutal reality of October 1917, but in Shostakovich's mind there was scant moral differentiation between the victims of tsarist repression and the later casualties of Communist terror. The change of calendar from Julian to Gregorian meant that the October Revolution actually happened in November, but the original date stuck. 'October' may have briefly stood as an emblem of liberty – the overthrow of the tsar was hailed by all shades of political opinion as signalling a potential revolution in human nature – but Shostakovich could only look back on 1917 with deep ambivalence. Official Soviet biographies placed the eleven-year-old Shostakovich at St Petersburg's Finland Station on 16 April of that charged year, allegedly watching the arrival of Lenin, returning from exile in Switzerland in his sealed train. Shostakovich himself either could not remember the moment or else feigned forgetfulness about his putative glimpse of the 'tyrant'; it seems too pat and convenient a detail, a way of legitimising an artist-hero's early biography. What is clear is that, all his life, he carried with him something that had happened when he was ten: the flash of a sabre on a city street and young blood suddenly spilt.

So impressive was Shostakovich's progress that in 1919 he was enrolled at the Petrograd Conservatory (St Petersburg's name had been changed five years earlier – at the start of the First World War – to something less German, more Russian sounding; not until 1924 was it renamed Leningrad) as its youngest matriculated student. He came under the wing of its director, composer Alexander Glazunov, who had reorganised the conservatory following the October Revolution. He brokered a good working relationship with the regime but was criticised for conservatism in his teaching and for his authoritarian approach to the students. Eventually, Glazunov took an opportunity afforded by the 1928 centenary of Franz Schubert's death. After attending the celebrations in Vienna, Glazunov did not so much defect as simply fail to go home. We don't know what impact he made on Shostakovich, who might well have shared his older compeers' doubts about Glazunov's aesthetics. He would have been aware that the director's teacher had been Rimsky-Korsakov, about whom Shostakovich himself had well-attested misgivings, which tempered his admiration and any clear artistic debt.

In the event, he studied piano with Leonid Nikolayev, but in the autumn he was allowed to join Maximilian Steinberg's composition class, having taken some private composition lessons in the summer. Steinberg was the son-in-law of Rimsky-Korsakov, who had died when Shostakovich was two, and so that early scherzo may have been as much flattery of a teacher as a genuine homage to the older composer. (Three years later, Shostakovich orchestrated Rimsky-Korsakov's *I Waited For Thee in the Grotto*, so there is no suggestion that he rejected the influence entirely; indeed, quite the opposite – it would have been hard to avoid Rimsky-Korsakov's dappled shadow.) He made rapid progress at the conservatory, watched over by Glazunov, who took an especially paternalistic interest in the young student's progress, which may well have reminded him of his own prodigious youth – and

doubtless of some of the problems attendant on it. Like Shostakovich, Glazunov had presented his First Symphony while
still a teenager and received the premiere audience's acclaim
wearing his school uniform. Inevitably, as with Shostakovich
later, rumours immediately circulated that the young man
'could not' have written a work of such maturity – a hurtful
imputation that bruised the tender-hearted Glazunov deeply.

In *Testimony* (and it may be one of the book's more reliable
sidebars), Shostakovich portrays Glazunov as a 'living legend'
but also perhaps as a figure of fun among the students; the
director still lived with his mother, who fussed around him
in cold weather and whenever he had a journey to make. The
conservatory students clearly considered him 'wet'. Shostakovich had reservations about the music too, dismissing the
symphonies as 'boring' – all development and no recapitulation or climax. One might draw certain connections between
this and Glazunov's perpetual bachelorhood, shackled to his
mother's apron strings. Certainly, one hears no tempestuous
emotion in Glazunov's music. Notwithstanding his sardonic
comments, Shostakovich had many reasons to be grateful. In
1920, Glazunov made him an award from the Borodin Fund
for young composers and, as previously mentioned, following a first attack of malnutrition two years later, Shostakovich
was granted extra rations at Glazunov's behest. The director
enjoyed good relations with the cultural commissar, Anatoly
Lunacharsky, and knew how to pull strings.

The 'signature' of a piano composer's work is almost always
conditioned by the size and shape of the hands: Ferruccio
Busoni and Sergei Rachmaninoff were both big men, and

their work reflects it. It's clear from Shostakovich's keyboard output that he did not possess the most generous stretch in his fingers. Those who heard him play in early life mention a dry accuracy rather than any expansiveness or great expressivity in his playing. It ought to be said that Shostakovich's emotional reticence and guardedness cannot simply be laid at the door of the Communist regime, as if ideological repression turned an open-hearted composer into a constrained and coded one. It might be argued, and with some justice, that Soviet conditions were merely a continuation of tsarist-era anxiety and paranoia, but it is also clear that Shostakovich was not temperamentally or physically equipped for the big gesture – at least not until the full orchestra became his palette – or open-hearted expression.

Fated by both genes and circumstance to be short in stature, he was seriously myopic, and his health was further undermined by Civil War shortages, despite the efforts of family and indulgent patrons like Glazunov to see that he was taken care of. The sudden death of his father in February 1922 was a further blow, in which grief and self-interest both played a part. It looked very much as though Shostakovich might have to give up his studies and find work to support the family. Sofiya, though, found employment as a cashier, while his sister Maria, who had recently completed her piano diploma, was able to earn a few roubles as an accompanist at the College of Choreography. The implication was either that Shostakovich's talent was too precious a thing to dilute with mundane work, or that he was not up to the rigours of bread-winning while maintaining his practice routine.

Despite the efforts of mother and sister, the family's circumstances remained precarious, however. Over the next two years, Shostakovich was obliged to seek work playing live accompaniment at the Bright Reel and other cinemas, most pressingly when Sofiya contracted malaria in the spring of 1924. That was the last year of Lenin's life. His successor, Joseph Stalin, had made many grand promises – planting a vast forest across the Siberian plains, building great canals, transforming the Russian economy wholesale – but draining the swamps came too late for Sofiya, who was permanently weakened by her infection. By then, Shostakovich had himself undergone a further bout of severe ill-health, diagnosed as tuberculosis, which had necessitated an expensive convalescence at Koreiz, a sanatorium in the Crimea (arranged by Glazunov, of course).

There were upsides to both of these experiences. Playing live accompaniment to silent films, at the very moment when cinema was seen as the cutting edge of Soviet modernism, was a bracing immersion in the zeitgeist; it expanded Shostakovich's expressive range considerably and reinforced in him a musical naturalism that had both satiric-comic and tragic dimensions. In addition, the Crimean sojourn threw him together with his first fiancée. His Preludes No. 6, No. 7, and No. 8, written in the early months of 1920, had been dedicated to Natasha Kuba, who is identified as his first girlfriend; the other pieces in the sequence were dedicated to Maria (No. 2 to No. 5), with the first dedicated to the artist Boris Kustodiev, who painted the thirteen-year-old Shostakovich's portrait that summer. Years later, in the Crimea, he met and became engaged to Tanya Glivenko. She was the daughter of a Moscow philologist who seems to have held some trustee capacity in the running of the sanatorium, allowing him to place Tanya and her sister there for the summer.

It is hard to imagine the awkward and obsessive Shostakovich being swept away by an affair of the heart, but he seems to have been captivated by the girl. Even so, who can judge whether, now that his piano studies were complete, his wish to move to Moscow to study composition under that ardent symphonist Nikolai Myaskovsky (Shostakovich's eventual output of fifteen symphonies hardly matches Myaskovsky's twenty-seven) was a considered career move or simply a desire to be close to Tanya? In the event, his mother intervened. He was persuaded to stay in Petrograd and complete his composition training with Steinberg. But the engagement continued for some six years; even after Tanya had married someone else, it seemed not-impossible that she would leave her husband and return to Shostakovich, who appears to have been able to inspire profound devotion in his female admirers. Only after the birth of Tanya's child did he accept the inevitable and marry Nina Vasilyevna Varzar instead. Not for the last time in his life did Shostakovich's unprepossessing exterior conceal a roil of competing passions. His emotional life was, if anything, more complex than his politics.

His Piano Trio No. 1 in C minor was dedicated to Tanya, but it was also his application piece for the free class at the Moscow Conservatory. Though fresher and less dense than his later writing – he was only sixteen, after all – it does not obviously sound like the work of a young man in love. The opening is a falling melody line that gradually builds over a heavy, repetitive figure, hinting at the grotesquerie that was to disturb Steinberg but was to become a defining characteristic of Shostakovich's mature music and the object of obsessive but mostly unresolved analysis. There is an unexpected hint of Rachmaninoff in the piano writing, a surprise given his apparent later dislike of that composer. However, it is hardly unusual to detect the anxiety of influence in a young composer. Sometimes imitation and rejection come hand-inglove. The miracle is how quickly Shostakovich assimilated and transcended his influences and moved beyond them.

The loss of his father had been a grievous blow, but by far the most serious fallout from the family's recent misfortunes and his own ill-health was the suspension of work on the symphony he had finished drafting around the beginning of 1923. This was to be the form in which his essence as a composer would be expressed, characterised by unflinching musical dialectic, a never-ending contention between formality and chaos, and a sharp duality of tragedy and satiric farce. It can, and often has, been argued that the symphonies represent the 'public' Shostakovich, the masked man, while the chamber music expresses the 'private' Shostakovich. It seems a false dichotomy. The great cycle of string quartets, only begun in 1938, is indeed intensely expressive and often personal, the works being musical inscapes in the manner of late Beethoven, Béla Bartók, and the 'autobiographical' string quartets of Leoš Janáček and Bedřich Smetana – but the symphonies are quintessentially personal too, even when Shostakovich seems to be playing an ambiguous, possibly even duplicitous, role.

In between these imagined poles lies the piano music, all the more personal because it was written for his own instrument, but also inherently public because it was the vehicle for Shostakovich's performing self. One of the many paradoxes of his nature was his commitment to performance, which became the outward shield of his inwardness. From the grief-stricken Suite in F-sharp minor for two pianos, written in memory of his father in 1923, to the great Bachian sequence of Twenty-Four Preludes, Op. 34, finished in 1933, the piano music covers the full spectrum of his compositional personality. There is another reason for its importance. While the teenage Shostakovich dreamed of joining Myaskovsky in Moscow and of writing symphonies, he was also the product of a virtual obsession with piano music and its performance, imposed on the Petrograd Conservatory (renamed Leningrad Conservatory in 1924) by its founder Anton Rubinstein. Seen as the only real rival among piano virtuosi to Franz Liszt, Rubinstein hid his own flagrant disregard for the notes as written behind a great wave of passionate 'expression', but insisted on accuracy as an absolute standard for conservatory students. Peter Ilich Tchaikovsky was one of his first significant students. It was a curious relationship: Tchaikovsky worshipped him; Rubinstein disliked his pupil. His more secure legacy was introducing the great European classics to American audiences in a series of money-spinning tours, permanently transforming musical tastes in the United States and paving the way for Shostakovich's brief lionisation during the war. However much he was a product of the Rubinstein establishment, and however much the present directorate insisted that his natural path was as a pianist-composer in the Lisztian mould (though this lineage required careful unpicking), Shostakovich was convinced that the symphony was his natural means of expression. Glazunov had met Liszt and, contrary to the usual impression of the Hungarian virtuoso as a shameless showman (see Ken Russell's manic film *Lisztomania* for a cleverly exaggerated portrayal of the Liszt cult), insisted that he played with accuracy and simplicity above all things. This, admittedly, was the later Liszt, largely retired from concert playing, but the point still went home: display of the Rubinstein sort was one thing, but there was a moral as well as aesthetic imperative to deliver the music as written.

The late winter of 1924 was to be Lenin's last. His death that January can hardly be said to have brought to an end an innocent golden age in Soviet Communism. As the philosopher Sidney Hook and others in the US argued, the emergent Stalinism was merely Leninism writ somewhat large, just as McCarthyism in the US was Trumanism writ small enough to infect a whole class. Lenin's era had been one of ruthless oppression and the violent 'cancelling' of opposition. Yet his death signalled the beginning of an inexorable change in Soviet politics, marked by internecine squabbling over succession to the revolutionary orb and sceptre, and the future course of international Communism itself. In the process, Leninism underwent a dialectical transformation into something darker still, a totalising politics that would haunt the remainder of Shostakovich's life, even after its main proponent had uneasily been pronounced dead. It is noteworthy that both Lenin and Stalin (and later leaders such as Leonid

Brezhnev, Konstantin Chernenko, and Yuri Andropov, representatives not so much of a gerontocracy as of a regime on life support) hovered uncertainly between death and life in their final days, the moment of actual departure occluded and hidden; even death had acquired a new semantics under the Soviets – you could be dead while still breathing and 'dead' to the world while still alive. Shostakovich was often described by observers as walking like a quickened corpse, 'mummified', or resembling a man recently removed from formaldehyde for public display – or, like Lenin, a waxen effigy.

The opposition of heroic Lenin and totalitarian Stalin is, of course, a Western myth, but Shostakovich and his fellow students had an immediate and ironic reminder of what was changing in the renaming of the city and its conservatory to Leningrad. An ideal revolutionary standard had been set, behind which almost anything could be perpetrated. Shostakovich resumed work on his symphonic sketches in October 1924. The family was still in hardship. Sofiya was ill and exhausted, and Shostakovich would continue to work as a cinema pianist until February of the following year, when three of his works (including the finished symphony and the Op. 11a Prelude for string octet, which was dedicated to his late friend Volodya Kurchavov) were published. Shostakovich had broken off work on his symphony to write a memorial to the young poet. That was not the only interruption: the previous month, Sofiya had been violently mugged outside her apartment block, a sign that all was not quite well in the socialist utopia. Despite these setbacks, Shostakovich worked doggedly and, on 1 July 1925, finished the score.

Symphony No. 1 in F minor was submitted and accepted for Shostakovich's composition diploma. It represents a brave and exceptional symphonic debut, far removed from the respectful homages and spring-like optimism that characterise most tyro symphonies. For a start, the work divides into two large blocks of radically different character. If there are strong influences at work – and it almost seems too acute and individual for that – they are Igor Stravinsky (and particularly the ballet *Petrushka*) in the opening two movements and the tragic world of Tchaikovsky in the final two. It is a work that may begin in the present but seems to end facing the past. The opening section alternates a march and a delicate waltz first heard on flute and woodwinds. There are early hints of the martial irruptions that represent Nazi invaders in the wartime symphonies or the forces of reaction and repression in the other ostensibly historically based works. Here, though, they seem to be little more than exercises in dramatic tension, timbre, and dynamic – though it's puzzling that a composer of Shostakovich's precocious talent should not have found a way to resolve such contentious material rather than simply stepping away from it. He did, after all, later criticise Glazunov for just such an inability to resolve his material. Perhaps something darker is betokened, even under such a playful surface.

The second movement is a true scherzo, again almost skittishly surreal. Significantly, it is the piano's first entrance that imposes some kind of order and sense of purpose to the material. Vivid orchestral outbreaks are interrupted by a songful trio just as they seem to be going somewhere, and then comes the first surprise: one commentator has likened the aural impact to the composer crumpling his score in disgust. Three vicious piano chords seem to call a halt to proceedings. The lower strings make a disgruntled response, and then three further chords – Stravinskian in dramatic effect – bring the movement to a sharp end.

Something fundamental has happened. If one looks for a programmatic explanation, the opening of the lento perhaps signifies childhood's end, or perhaps the fading of innocent political hope. The mood now seems unrelievedly pessimistic and brooding. Oboe and cello try to find some relief, but once more there is a blunt opposition between a fiercely martial section (trumpet and war drums) and further humane calls from oboe, clarinet, and violin. Again, the material does not so much reach a conclusion as simply disembody.

The stage is thereby set for an upbeat and affirmative finale. It is, instead, blunt and disorderly, indifferent in every way to further woodwind calls. Piano again helps to impose some kind of structure and the first great melody in Shostakovich's work slowly emerges, most distinctly stated by solo violin. The music builds in power and authority until it comes hard up against the fatalistic conclusion of the lento movement, restated fortissimo on the kettledrums, but this time in the form of a question. There is some attempt to provide a response, but the weight of the military figure is now too strong, and it brings the symphony to a darkly chastened conclusion.

With hindsight, and according to one's preference for a strictly technical over a psychological interpretation, there are many ways of judging Symphony No. 1 in F minor: as a bold technical exercise that could not be maintained, or that might seem too bold in a diploma piece to be tactically sound; as a sharp rejection of modernist ironies (those mechanistic themes and procedures in the first two movements) and a retreat into history; as a strikingly honest representation of Shostakovich's own recent experience of youthful irresponsibility pulled up short by bereavement, hunger, hard work, and intimations of his own mortality; or as a parable of recent Russian history, or rather a reverse parable, with the forces of collectivism having to face up to an inexorable fate, a kind of 'return of the repressed'.

As so often with Shostakovich, the work is capacious enough to sustain any number of contradictory interpretations. What is immediately clear is that the young composer is in complete command of his material, even when he appears not to be, and that he has a clear understanding of its perverse trajectory. Glazunov immediately recognised the symphony's quality and arranged to have the work performed. Shostakovich himself may have drawn as much satisfaction from being able to travel to Moscow to play a piano reduction of the score for Myaskovsky but, exactly a fortnight earlier, on 12 May 1926, Nikolai Malko conducted the premiere in St Petersburg. 'I acquired a certain fame', Shostakovich noted laconically. For all its callow contradictions of tone, the First Symphony was an immediate hit with critics and audiences. (Malko, who emigrated in 1929, also conducted the premiere of Symphony No. 2 in 1927, and later did much to promote Shostakovich's reputation abroad.) Shostakovich took four curtain calls at the first performance. His youth was noted but, unlike Glazunov, he was not obliged to take the applause wearing a gymnasium uniform, which somewhat protected him from charges that other, older hands must be responsible. Why would anyone think so? Whatever else it may be, the First Symphony is unmistakably a young man's work.

Not for another eight years, with the premiere of his opera *Lady Macbeth of Mtsensk*, would Shostakovich enjoy a similar success. On that later occasion, though, the victory would be temporary, even pyrrhic, and would mark the real beginning of his bizarre and troubled relationship with the man who had picked up Lenin's torch and taken obsessive charge of every aspect of Soviet politics and culture. The public may have enjoyed Shostakovich's opera, but Joseph Stalin loathed it, and the leader's critical disapproval could be fatal.

Two

After Shostakovich died in 1975, almost half a century after the brilliant premiere of his Symphony No. 1 in F minor, the Soviet government put out a statement hailing his work as 'a remarkable example of fidelity to the traditions of musical classicism'. The communiqué lapses into more familiar rhetoric thereafter, mentioning Shostakovich's contributions to 'socialist realism', his unflinchingly realistic approach to Russian life and traditions, and his contribution to 'universal progressive musical culture'. However hollow the whole tribute may have sounded, given the many tendentious issues that surrounded his work and all the critical vagaries that greeted it, the first part of that statement cannot be faulted.

It is already possible, even this early in the story, to offer a general description of Shostakovich's music. Few great artists in any form have shown such consistency of purpose, a perception that, while useful, tends to confound a critical consensus that Shostakovich was forced into time-serving (and life-saving) compromise throughout his working life. Any extensive survey of his work in score, in performance, and on record, points to a singleness of vision. It is not a career that divides easily into 'periods', other than those dictated by external circumstance, and while there is considerable variation in Shostakovich's writing between and within differ-ent genres – string quartets, piano music, vocal music, opera, the symphony – all of it, nearly 150 separate opuses, is driven by the same adamantine logic. 'Fidelity' and 'classicism' may seem curious words to find in an official Soviet statement, but they are absolutely pertinent.

Shostakovich was fated to be dismissed as old-fashioned by Western critics in thrall to the modernism of the Second Viennese School, and as suspiciously newfangled by his com-patriots. He was to a degree Janus-faced – not in his political sympathies, which remained constant, but in his simultaneous modernity and traditionalism. Though he dabbled later with elements of the dodecaphonic approach once condemned as anti-musical, his use of it was fiercely circumscribed by clas-sical tonality; String Quartet No. 12 and his final symphony, No. 15, both use a tone row but are cast in D flat and C major, the key of classical affirmation, respectively. Unlike Stravin-sky, who went through a 'serialist' period influenced by his American amanuensis Robert Craft, Shostakovich only rarely and reluctantly parted from tonality. He made free use of the violently dissonant harmonies that had become part of the language of twentieth-century music, but only in such a way that answered the harmonic teleology of the defining key sig-nature. Much of the violent drama and acerbic satire heard in his work is actually the function of easily identified musical procedures and does not need any extraneous explanation, let alone an agonised battle of conscience between ideological correctness and heresy. And yet, from his Second Symphony onward, Shostakovich's work was subjected to intense non-musical scrutiny, its themes, message, tone, literalness or sarcasm, sincerity or artifice being argued over with rare ferocity. The paradox of the music's highly 'personal' nature and its technical rigour is one that any student of Shostakovich has to confront and that none can hope to resolve easily, if at all.

Before considering the Second Symphony, it is worth pausing for a moment to consider the comments of two other distinguished composers. At the height of Shostakovich's fame, in 1944, Arnold Schoenberg wrote to Kurt List, editor of *Listen: The Guide to Good Music*, thanking him for copies of articles about himself and about Shostakovich. The implication is that the latter article was at least in part negative, for Schoenberg seems to follow his thanks by jumping to the Russian's defence:

> I still think Shostakovich is a great talent. It is perhaps
> not his fault that he has allowed politics to influence
> his compositorial [sic] style. And even if it is a weakness
> in his character – he might be no hero, but a talented
> musician. In fact, there are heroes, and there are
> composers. Heroes can be composers and vice versa, but
> you cannot require it.

At the height of the war against Hitler and fascism – Schoenberg was writing from his distant exile in California – Shostakovich had been pressed into service as both hero and composer. The helmeted figure, captioned 'Fireman Shostakovich', who appeared on the 20 July 1942 edition of *Time* magazine, was understood to be a powerful spokesman for his country's political ideals and the chief musical celebrant of its historical achievements. The Shostakovich illustrated by Boris Artzybasheff on that *Time* cover looks improbably chivalric or Roman, and the musical staves that float above his head like wisps of smoke are a curiously bathetic touch in light of the burning, shattered buildings in the background. Schoenberg's comment – 'a weakness in his character' – has been echoed down the years in line with the assumption that Shostakovich willingly or at best self-protectively subordinated his art to the service of the Soviet Union and its rapidly changing policies. His 'heroism' was as fragile a concept as the wartime alliance of East and West.

Here, though, is another comment about Shostakovich from a distinguished fellow musician. Though it relates to a much later work, it has profound bearing on all of Shostakovich's work from the Second Symphony onward. British composer Michael Tippett's longevity makes it easy to forget that he was a near contemporary of the Russian – Tippett was born in January 1905 and died in 1998 – while the anthropological obsessions of his operas and the pictorial elegance of late works like *The Rose Lake* obscure the committed leftism of his earlier years. Though resistant to dogma, the young Tippett was a socialist through and through, so his perspective on Shostakovich is worth canvassing. As quoted by his companion and amanuensis Meirion Bowen, Tippett mentions that Symphony No. 11 is 'supposed to be' concerned with the events of the 1905 revolution: 'I was quite sure when I heard it that the use of 1905 *was a kind of political alibi*, since this was a matter of known revolutionary history. The music to me *was self-evidently about Shostakovich's own experiences in the catastrophe of his life*' (emphasis my own).

Therein lie the key questions that go to the root of Shostakovich's life and work. In what sense was his life a 'catastrophe'? And what do we understand by 'meaning' in instrumental or orchestral music – and specifically political meaning? Can we talk about 'subject'? Must a work that bears a poetic title be heard differently to one that merely carries an opus number? How do verbal and musical meaning relate? Or what can we infer from the juxtaposition of certain words and certain sounds? And, underneath it all, how do we excavate the composer's 'real' intention?

The year 1927 marked a new epoch in Soviet Communism and in Shostakovich's life. In October, against all odds, Russians celebrated the tenth anniversary of the Bolshevik Revolution. The regime had survived civil war, foreign intervention, famine, various internal 'counter-revolutionary' initiatives, and a fierce power struggle that would lead to the expulsion of Leon Trotsky and Grigory Zinoviev and the introduction of Stalin's nationalist programme of 'socialism in one country', a seeming abandonment of the internationalist programme of socialism.

Exactly one week before the United Opposition was purged, on 5 November, Shostakovich's Symphony No. 2 in B major was premiered in Leningrad. It was a time of profound change for the young composer. He had been accepted for a higher degree and would remain a postgraduate student until July 1928. He had, some months before, destroyed his juvenilia, a conventional enough gesture, but a clear sign that he now had a clear image of what kind of composer he wanted to become. In April 1927, he met the brilliant, seemingly omniscient polymath Ivan Sollertinsky, who was to become arguably the closest friend of his life and a significant intellectual influence. He also met the woman who would become his first wife, Nina Vasilyevna Varzar, the daughter of well-off parents and a natural philosophy student; their engagement came two years later.

Shostakovich's personal horizons seemed to be widening. As he took a break from composition following the success of his First Symphony, he began to spread his wings as a performer. The only major piece written in this period was, significantly, a virtuosic keyboard work, the fiendish Piano Sonata No. 1, a work that later fell under official censure. At the end of January, shortly after premiering the sonata in Moscow, he had performed in the First International Chopin Competition in Warsaw. Though he didn't win, the subsequent tour took him through Poland and to Berlin, where he met the conductor Bruno Walter, an important champion of his work in Europe, as Leopold Stokowski was to be in America. In November, Walter conducted Shostakovich's First Symphony in Berlin, just over two weeks after his Symphony No. 2 in B major was premiered in Leningrad.

The latter is immediately and strikingly different from its predecessor. It is written in a single movement but, more intriguingly, for the first time, it bears a programmatic title and concludes on a choral part with text. The First Symphony is usually analysed on technical and structural grounds, because it remains susceptible to such analysis. The Second is more textural in conception, and has led to comparison with the gestural painting of the American abstract expressionists, a more-than-usually significant comparison given more recent revelations about the way Jackson Pollock, Willem De Kooning and others were internationally marketed (there's no other word) as evidence of American freedom and individualism – the opposite of Soviet dogmatism, intellectual constraint, and expressive control.

But perhaps more important than the symphony's technical innovations is the question of meaning, of the composer's non-musical intentions and affiliations. As ever, this is a minefield. As a subtitle, *To October* seems conventional enough for a Soviet composer of the time – Eisenstein's film *October: Ten Days That Shook the World* was being shown around the same time – and the choral text could not be more conventionally affirmative. By 1927, the Marxist mantra 'Proletarians of all countries, unite!', which is also affixed to the script, was as ubiquitous and unconsidered as 'Drink Coca-Cola' in the West. Revisionist biographers and critics have tried to suggest that Shostakovich's title – he had apparently also considered calling the First Piano Sonata *October Symphony* – does not refer specifically to the Bolshevik Revolution but to a more abstract spirit of democracy and a promise of freedom which Shostakovich already considered to be betrayed. To be sure, his political sympathies were more fully engaged by the revolution of 1905, to which Symphony No. 11 was dedicated. (Interestingly, the poet and novelist Boris Pasternak, whose career in some measure parallels Shostakovich's but who was then very much a favoured writer, chose the occasion of the tenth anniversary of the Bolshevik ascendancy to publish his epic poem *The Year 1905*.) To some extent, such titles are gestural. Almost every writer, artist, and musician in the Soviet Union was producing texts that invoked revolutionary history and spirit, and the Second Symphony was written on commission from Muzsektor, the music division of the state publishing house, Gosizdat, overseen by Stalin's cultural commissar, Anatoly Lunacharsky. It may be that, at twenty-one, Shostakovich liked the idea of being a composer laureate to the new regime and was prepared to subordinate his own convictions to Communist rhetoric. Or it may have been the composer's first tentative step towards constructing the creative 'alibi' Tippett refers to, camouflaging a private drama with public gestures.

It is interesting that in Shostakovich's memoir, *Testimony* – though any reference to the book must be guarded with qualifications – when the composer refers to the frightening street disturbances of 1917 and the moment when he saw the young boy cut down in the street, he immediately afterward makes reference to the sex workers who plied St Petersburg's main avenue, Nevsky Prospekt, and his fear of them. The text, authored in fact by Solomon Volkov, may be a faithful representation of Shostakovich's freely associated and dictated memories, but that makes the juxtaposition all the more interesting: sexual anxiety and shyness – a small boy attracting the 'motherly' but discomfiting attentions of sex workers – set immediately against the political unrest that was turning the country upside down.

Whether the words are Shostakovich's own or Volkov's clever ventriloquism, there is a further passage in *Testimony* that precisely addresses the question of meaning in music and sets it in the broadest cultural context. Shostakovich concedes that the issue might sound strange to someone raised in the West:

> It's here in Russia that the question is usually posed: What was the composer trying to say, after all, with this musical work? What was he trying to make clear? The questions are naive, of course, but despite their naivete and crudity, they definitely merit being asked. And I would add to them, for instance: Can music attack evil? Can it make man stop and think?

When, in 1936, Shostakovich vociferously denied the then-routine charge of formalism, it was less on personal grounds than from a deep, almost genetic conviction that art conceived purely as form and without some moral content was a chimera. Long before Stalinism or socialist realism, there was a deep didactic strain in Russian art. The political reliability or otherwise of the intellectuals – a principle known as *(ne)blagonadyozhny* – had been an urgent question for the regime since the reign of Catherine the Great. That context in no way invalidates Tippett's suggestion that Shostakovich used politics as a kind of front; though Russian to the depths of his being, he also understood that art was the expression of a soul and not some abstract collectivity. There, and not in Communism-vs-anti-Communism, lies the paradox of Shostakovich.

The Second Symphony is a strange work, not because it bears a 'political' or 'historical' subtext but because its music is strange. It is, in reality, a cantata, subsequently renamed as a symphony and commissioned to include a tub-thumping panegyric to Lenin by the Komsomol poet Alexander Bezymensky. Its self-consciousness is (to borrow from the infamous superscription of the Fifth Symphony, written a decade later) the creative reply of a Soviet artist to just (or unjust) criticism, an incongruous blend of experimental writing and crude agitprop. That may very well explain why in later years Shostakovich effectively disclaimed it, along with the Third Symphony; he asked his son, Maxim, a conductor, for a promise not to conduct either work. The criticism came from within the new Soviet cultural establishment. In a sour foretaste of what was to come in the 1930s, the Russian Association of Proletarian Musicians (RAPM), a creative union, had criticised the First Symphony's dependence on the romantic individualism of Tchaikovsky and other 'bourgeois' composers. The Westward-looking rival Association for Contemporary Music, meanwhile, warned that he ran the risk of seeming out of date.

In response, Shostakovich wrote a work that is almost onomatopoeically responsive to the times. It is hard to recover the atmosphere of post-revolutionary Russia. The Western caricature of Russia and Russians as dour, unsmiling, ascetic, and slavishly obedient to authority is little more than that, or no more than an extrapolation from later circumstances. For a period in the 1920s, a hectic moral anarchy reigned, more libertine than libertarian. The overthrow of bourgeois authority stretched into private life – sexual freedom was preached, divorce and abortion sanctioned – and ultimately into art as well. Experimentalism, later to become the object of official anathema, was all. 'Biomechanics' was the fashionable retort to romantic love, altruism, principled action; we are as machines, it proclaims, as driven as any industrial engine or motor car; reason is an illusion. The poet Vladimir Mayakovsky, a kind of literary punk happy to parrot official anathema and spit vitriol at more talented figures, became the darling of the revolution and, in turn, the most prominent victim of its habitual cycle of favour and disfavour. In 1929, Shostakovich wrote incidental music for Mayakovsky's play *The Bedbug*, an overheated critical disaster. After the further failure of *The Bathhouse* the following year, Mayakovsky shot himself. It was a symbolic end to the old decade. His reputational rehabilitation by Stalin as the 'greatest' and 'most gifted' just five years later was one of the perversities of the new one.

Shostakovich's Second Symphony is not a field recording, but it captures a mood with disconcerting precision. Almost entirely abstract and themeless, it studiously avoids the expressive inscape and tragic conclusion of the First Symphony. It tells no story, unless the wild juxtaposition of separate lines is intended to reflect the ideological morass out of which the Bolshevik Party rose, triumphant and strong. Or, in the inevitable alternative view, do those same passages reflect the wild amorality and unregulated self-definition that followed the revolution, however briefly? There is no answer, just as there is no way of making an absolute judgement about the work's apparently dominant influence. If Stravinsky and Tchaikovsky, respectively, stood over the two halves of the First Symphony, its successor seems haunted by the work of the composer Alexander Scriabin, who had posthumously – Scriabin died in 1915, aged just forty-three – been declared sound and affirmative by Lunacharsky. Is that the point? Was Shostakovich kowtowing to official tastes and prescriptions? Or was he sarcastically celebrating a composer whose 'mystic chords', theatrical aura, and theosophical pretensions he instinctively despised?

A bleak, slow passage for strings follows, and then there is a restatement, on clarinet, of the theme from the youthful *Funeral March for the Victims of the Revolution*. This high part, an atonal fugato, is the only clear-cut thematic writing in the entire work, and it will appear again in Symphony No. 12 with its subtitle *The Year 1917*. The deep structure of Shostakovich's musical imagination starts to reveal itself.

And then the choir comes in, singing of Lenin and struggle, the forging of a destiny out of despair. It's hard to hear the finale as anything other than Bolshevik propaganda. Shostakovich, of course, did not write the words; he professed to loathe them, and he treats them with curious disregard in his setting. The text was given to him by Bezymensky, the poet and writer-in-residence with the Leningrad Working Youth Theatre; in return, Shostakovich agreed to act as its musical director, another potential 'cover' post. Given the literary associations he was making, which would soon impact strongly on his life and career, one would have thought Shostakovich could have found a more distinguished text. On the other hand, he was pressed for time and always aware of Muzsektor watching over his shoulder for any signs of bourgeois self-indulgence.

There is a simple, knot-cutting explanation for Shosta-kovich's later disavowal of the Second Symphony: it is not very good. Like many artists who achieve runaway success with a first major work – one thinks of the young Ameri-can novelist he met in New York in 1949 who struggled to equal the success of *The Naked and the Dead*, following it with *Barbary Shore*, a forced and airless fictionalisation of his Waldorf-Astoria 'plague on both your houses' intervention – Shostakovich seemed emptied out and directionless. Such a man is clearly susceptible to external influences, particularly if they carry a certain promise of professional security. Such factors notwithstanding, Shostakovich seemed to be going through a transformation – not sloughing a skin, but adding a new and impenetrable one.

He returned to symphonic writing two years later and rattled off his Symphony No. 3 in E-flat major in less than a month. Unlike the Second Symphony, it was not written to a commission. Like its predecessor, though, it is a single-movement work with a historical subtitle (*The First of May*) and a choral finale, this time after a poem by Semyon Kirsanov. It has the same vocalised quality and the same audio-vérité impression of shouting voices, milling crowds, and a mixture of hectic enthusiasm and deep dread. The music critic Ian MacDonald, a shrewd observer of Shostako-vich, suggests that the first aural intimations of nemesis can be heard in the work. If so, there is an irony in the circum-stances of its creation, for Shostakovich finished his score while staying at a Black Sea resort in Georgia, only a score or so versts distant from the birthplace of Joseph Vissarionovich

Djugashvili, the one-time brigand who now ran the Soviet Union under his revolutionary soubriquet: Stalin. Whether one really can hear 'the Man of Steel' in the clanking brass and rumbling strings of the Third Symphony is a less interesting question than where one locates Shostakovich in it. It is, at least on the surface, an orthodox Communist symphony, written at the composer's own behest and under no apparent duress. Whether it is something else below the surface is a moot point. Shostakovich later dismissed both his Second and Third Symphonies as instances of some kind of 'infantile disorder', as if they were chickenpox or scarlet fever, inconveniences to be overcome rather than creative successes. They also attracted the dread word 'experimental', which was a bête noire in Soviet aesthetics of the time. The idea that the end result could not be known in advance did not sit well with the iron logic of dialectical materialism.

MacDonald also cites the English critic Gerald Abraham, who in *Eight Soviet Composers* describes his inescapable feeling, listening to the Third Symphony, that Shostakovich 'is playing a part ... He tries to be Marxian, but fantastic Gogolian humour keeps breaking in'. Nikolai Gogol's capacious novel *Dead Souls* is perhaps his most important work, but his story 'The Nose' is undoubtedly more famous – an example of the Russian interest in surreal fauna, like Mayakovsky's bedbug or Mikhail Bulgakov's talking cat, but a step beyond and into a realm where body parts detach and take on lives of their own. Abraham's comment is doubly perceptive. It underscores MacDonald's central thesis about Shostakovich, and Michael Tippett's: that he donned a self-protective armour of apparent orthodoxy and compliance, through the chinks in which one glimpses a whole battery of contradictory emotions and attitudes – satire, rancour, self-pity, self-aggrandisement, harsh laughter, pathos, an irrepressible humanism, all the way to overt *anti*-Communism. Sarcastic overstatement – or *vranyo* – is a favourite Russian rhetorical device. Where, say, a French anti-clerical writer might launch a frontal assault on the Church, replete with exaggerated accusations of simony, nepotism, greed, drunkenness, and sexual perversion, a Russian would be more inclined to subvert religious or secular authority by an affectation of absurd piety or orthodoxy. Perhaps Shostakovich's 'Communist' hymns and paeans are exaggerated with satiric intent.

Something else, even more profoundly subversive, may be at work. MacDonald, Volkov, and, by implication, Abraham all persuasively align Shostakovich with the ancient principle of *yurodstvo*. MacDonald's summary of it cannot be bettered:

> The *yurodivy* or 'holy fool' is a venerable Russian tradition whereby anyone wishing to mock the mighty may do so with relative impunity *provided they behave in all other aspects as if unworthy of serious attention* [my italics]. The parallel with the English court jester is more or less exact and it is significant that the Fool in *King Lear* was, after Hamlet, Shostakovich's favourite Shakespearian creation.

Much has been made of Shostakovich's resemblance to Hamlet – his prevarication, procrastination, self-doubt, even his affectation of insanity when he seemed to defy the Claudius-like

Soviet regime. It is an analogy that broke down somewhat when the Nazi Fortinbras was battering at the Russian gates. Did he play the Fool? Was it his fated role to lead the gerontocracy across the wasted Cold War heath, soaking up blows but being the only one with clear vision? The trap for Shostakovich lay in an important qualification made by MacDonald, italicised in my quotation. Had he passed his career writing satirical songs to be sung in bars or drawing rooms, as his father had done, he might well have acted with impunity. But Shostakovich became a symphonist and operatic composer of international fame who attracted the most serious attention. Even if he was considered to be a *yurodivy* – and, Volkov states explicitly, that was no retrospective notion but the general view during Shostakovich's lifetime – he exposed himself to enormous risk.

Thus far, Shostakovich's career had been crowned with success and official approval. There were, however, profound changes afoot in his self-perception and creative persona. Abraham very exactly identified their source. Immediately after finishing the Second Symphony, Shostakovich had begun work on an opera. If the symphonies had brought him academic recognition and official approval, he now seemed determined to produce a trickster work – frivolous, throwaway, double-wrapped in irony, and impenetrable as to meaning and intention. At the simplest level, *The Nose* is a homage to a favourite writer. It is based on Gogol's story, which Shostakovich read avidly in his teens. The plot is scanty in the extreme. A bumptious tsarist official, Major Kovalyov, wakens to find that his nose has gone off on its own and

is enjoying the privileges and exerting some of the responsibilities of the major's new office. There is a chase, and the
nose is eventually restored to its proper position and function.
Much pseudo-psychoanalytic ink has been spilled in arguing
a psycho-sexual interpretation of both story and opera. Such
approaches work for Philip Roth's 1970s mammary fantasy,
The Breast, but they run aground on the deliberate thinness
of Gogol's narrative, and Shostakovich's librettists' rather different version of it. What is important in both is the tone:
dismissive, abrupt, more interested in the cadence of speech
than in what is actually said. That there is less to *The Nose* than
meets the eye (so to speak!) is almost exactly what it is about.

At a personal level, the opera is influenced by the playful
intelligence of Ivan Sollertinsky. It also derives something
from the 'biomechanical' theories of the theatre director
Vsevolod Meyerhold, with whom Shostakovich was working
in Moscow in the spring of 1928. The immediate spark was
seeing the first Russian production of Alban Berg's opera
Wozzeck at the Mariinsky Theatre in Leningrad the previous
year. The work seemed to reflect something of Meyerhold's
mechanistic approach to character. Some have suggested that
the absurdist, anti-realistic tone of *The Nose* was in part influenced by Sergei Prokofiev's *The Love of Three Oranges*, which
had premiered in Chicago in 1921 but received its first Russian
performance, also at the Mariinsky, on 18 February 1926, to
enthusiastic acclaim (and persistent argument about whether
the correct title contains 'of' or 'for'). Shostakovich only
met the older composer the following February, but there was
a connection through Meyerhold, a supporter of both: the

basis for Prokofiev's opera had been an adaptation of Carlo Gozzi's eighteenth-century fairy tale *L'amore delle tre melarance* ('the love of three oranges') written by none other than Meyerhold, who used the same title for his journal devoted to the study of commedia dell'arte. (The moonstruck protagonist of Arnold Schoenberg's *Pierrot Lunaire*, a work admired by Shostakovich, also derives from commedia.) The jester theme of *The Love of Three Oranges*, its clash between magic (dogma?) and laughter, and its premise in the prince's chronic hypochondria seem to anticipate those of *The Nose* and Shostakovich's evolving *yurodivy* role, as does what Prokofiev's biographer Harlow Robinson characterises as the 'aggressively stylised … and artificial' tone of the piece. The same words could be used to describe *The Nose*.

Shostakovich's work was given a concert performance in June 1929, amid considerable controversy, and then fully staged in January 1930, within twenty-four hours of the Third Symphony's premiere. The opera's reception established a pattern: popular with the public, who flocked to more than a dozen performances at the Maly Opera Theatre in Leningrad; disliked by the musical watchdogs of RAPM, who objected to the work's lack of foundation in contemporary Soviet reality.

That reality was changing fast. Trotsky and Nikolai Bukharin were gone. The Soviet Union had entered a period of enforced collectivisation and 'superindustrialisation' under the first Five-Year Plan. A cultural revolution that subordinated all expressive freedom and individuality to the needs of the party was in progress. All art was to be proletarianised. A *Pravda* article by the country's new leader declared 1917 to have been a cultural 'year zero'. The poet Vladimir Mayakovsky offered the perfect metaphor for the creative artist's new situation when he took to playing Russian roulette: the act of publishing new creative work was a spin of the cylinder. The click of an empty chamber was perhaps the best an artist could hope for: bathetic, but officially sanctioned. Shostakovich had his first serious taste of official disapproval, but had perhaps found a protective disguise as Pierrot, Harlequin, and Fool.

Others were not so lucky. Meyerhold was a prominent victim of the Soviet regime's about-turn on experimentalism and the avant-garde. His work was declared to be alien to Soviet realities, and the Meyerhold Theatre was closed in 1938. A year later, he was arrested, and a 'confession' was obtained from him under torture. Meyerhold bravely withdrew it in court. He was executed by firing squad on 1 or 2 February 1940. Sollertinsky's end was less dramatic, but the loss was no less grievous for Shostakovich. His friend – arguably his only real friend – succumbed to a heart attack at home in Novosibirsk, shortly before taking up a chair at the Moscow Conservatory, a post that would have brought him closer to his old friend. In grief, Shostakovich wrote the Piano Trio No. 2 in E minor, a work that requires absolutely no effort of interpretation, brimming with pain.

Finally, to Prokofiev. He had lived in Paris and worked abroad since 1920 but had been consistently admired at home. He visited Russia in 1927 and again in 1929, when his dissonant 'industrial ballet' *Le pas d'acier* was performed at Moscow's Beethoven Hall. A symphonic suite derived from the theatre work had been programmed in Moscow the previous year, to some acclaim, but admiration was more than usually fickle during the cultural revolution. RAPM condemned *Le pas d'acier* as counter-revolutionary and hypothetically fascist. Prokofiev returned to Paris in a rage.

Shostakovich never seems to have contemplated exile, let alone defection, with any seriousness. One wonders what his life and work might have been like if he had slipped his New York handlers at the Waldorf Astoria and declared a wish to live in the West. Counterfactuals are always fascinating, if a little redundant, but in Shostakovich's case they throw up something with absolute clarity: it is almost impossible to imagine him living anywhere but in the embrace of Mother Russia. His inconsistent diatribes against Prokofiev and Stravinsky have much to do with their decisions to leave the country. Prokofiev did eventually return to live in Russia from 1932, and his career and Shostakovich's ran in intriguingly different directions for the next two decades. During the fraught and difficult mid-1930s, when Shostakovich wrestled with his problematic Fourth and Fifth Symphonies, Prokofiev seemed content to write songs and political cantatas – including one to mark the twentieth anniversary of the Bolshevik Revolution, which was scored for choruses, military bands, folksy accordions, and percussion, and whose lyrics incorporated texts by the great triumvirate of Soviet Communism. The work wasn't performed at the time and was only heard in 1966, with one of the texts pointedly removed. Prokofiev lived on, internationally famous, trying to please the regime and criticised for it. His *Hymn to the Soviet Union* failed to win a wartime competition for a new national anthem; a song by

Alexander Alexandrov, even more shamelessly patriotic, was chosen instead. Robinson points out that 'as Prokofiev's music was becoming more "public", Shostakovich's was becoming more "private". While Prokofiev would write the explicitly nationalistic music for [Eisenstein's film] *Alexander Nevsky* in 1938, Shostakovich would write his First String Quartet.' Prokofiev died in his bed on 5 March 1953 – the same day, as far as anyone can tell, as the death of the man whose words would later be edited out of that revolutionary anniversary cantata, the man who had ruled the Soviet Union for the past quarter century.

Three

As a pianist, Shostakovich knew that the key to men's souls is not their eyes – his own shifted uneasily behind pebble-thick spectacles – but their hands. When he met Joseph Stalin, he saw before him 'an ordinary, shabby little man, short, fat, with reddish hair. His face was covered with pockmarks and his right hand was noticeably thinner than his left. He kept hiding his right hand'. The pockmarks were airbrushed out of propaganda photographs, and on public occasions Stalin wore elevator shoes and stood on a small platform to raise him to a more heroic height. Only a few knew that the leader also had a webbed left foot, which would in itself have made him an object of suspicion in superstitious Russia. There is a wealth of subtle malice in Shostakovich's description – which comes, inevitably, from *Testimony* – and just a tinge of 'bio-mechanical' symbolism. Had that hand become withered signing death warrants? Was it hidden out of guilt or guile?

Stalin ruled by intimidation. He is perhaps the greatest mass murderer of history, a dubious accolade that resists confirmation, since no one will ever know how many died in cellars or in mass graves on his orders, or how many uncensused and illiterate peasants were systematically starved to death in accordance with his decrees. Hitler, too, hid a tremulous paretic hand behind his back, but he at least maintained a few loyalties to the very end and reserved some affection for friends and family members. Stalin spared no one; today's friend was tomorrow's inconvenience. Hitler may have put some squeamish distance between himself and the consequences of his edicts. Stalin did no such thing. The 'Red Tsar' overturned Nicholas I's famous – but possibly apocryphal, and attributed to different tsars at different times – comment that Russia was ruled not by him but by his 10,000 clerks. Stalin was what nowadays would be called a micromanager. He may have been a philistine – indeed, his use of culture as a political tool confirms it – but it was clear from the very beginning of the revolution that the arts, which always had a didactic dimension in Russian culture, would be harnessed by the regime and put to political ends.

It is well known that Hitler's supposed passion for Richard Wagner's work disguised a preference for light operetta; most matters of high culture were left to the aesthete Joseph Goebbels. Stalin's real tastes were no more sophisticated, and they were largely satisfied by the little film-screening room in the Kremlin where the entire Politburo was often required to sit alongside him – or, rather, in the seats behind his private row – and watch either the latest release or an old favourite. According to Shostakovich, 'Stalin loved films and he saw *The Great Waltz*, about Johann Strauss, many times, dozens of times … [he] also liked Tarzan films'. Johnny Weissmuller's movies notwithstanding, Stalin considered himself a man of taste and discrimination and amply qualified to meddle in the music of a man like Shostakovich.

They make a curious pair, the dictator and the composer, but for the next twenty years J. V. Stalin and D. D. Shostakovich were to observe the steps of a strange and very Russian dance, its choreography an awkward blend of ideology and principle, its metre irregular, its course along the edge of a precipice. Shostakovich may have hinted at Stalin's presence in the clanking cadences of the Second Symphony. He later adapted Mussorgsky's work *Rayok* as a satirical cantata titled *The Little Antiformalistic Paradise*, a skit on the directives of Stalin's cultural commissar, Andrei Zhdanov, and on the regime as a whole. It was begun in 1948, while Stalin was still alive, but only completed in 1957, after his death. Stalin is cast as Edinitsyn, which means 'number one' but also 'the dunce'. It's a sign that, however 'harsh and intolerant' he may have seemed (and that is his own description of his younger self), Shostakovich had a sense of humour and a great sense of fun, and he was by all accounts a fiendish poker player. Keeping a poker face was a good survival strategy in Soviet Russia.

It is important to distinguish between the stressed and undernourished Shostakovich who visited America after the Second World War and the twenty-four-year-old who had recovered from most of his childhood and teenage ills and was being bruited about as the up-and-coming man in Russian, or Soviet, music. Isaac Glikman, who became Shostakovich's friend and secretary in the 1930s, described him as looking younger than his years:

I was captivated by the refinement of his face, its individuality, its noble aspect ... In many early descriptions, Shostakovich is depicted as physically weak, frail, and even puny, but these are extremely misleading statements. In my view, Shostakovich was of decent height, slender, yet supple and strong. His clothes always suited him ... His head was crowned with wonderful dark copper-coloured hair, which was carefully combed, or else fell in poetic disorder.

Here is a description to set alongside Shostakovich's thumbnail sketch of Stalin! The key word in it is 'captivated'. Even those who sensed a troubled soul behind the wise grey eyes, or who saw the floppy fringe as part of his camouflage, were instinctively impressed. This was the forceful young man who married Nina Vasilyevna Varzar in May 1932 and forged a relationship so strong, for all its volatility, that the couple remarried immediately after their divorce in the spring of 1935 and started a family: their daughter, Galina, came a year later, and the future conductor, Maxim, two years after that.

To hear Shostakovich's music as uniformly dark and tragic without an appreciation of its moments of comedy – black or lighter – distorts it every bit as much as to consider it monolithically 'pro-Soviet' or 'anti-Communist'. His insistence that *The Nose* should be heard as a horror story rather than a comedy was, of course, partly tongue-in-cheek, the *yurodivy* concealing his real meaning. Between the work's concert and stage premieres, the country had just celebrated Stalin's fiftieth birthday, the beginnings of the 'cult of personality' later denounced by Nikita Khrushchev. Few among the opera's audience could have missed the humour or horror of Gogol's parable, or indeed whom Shostakovich intended with his characterisation of the runaway organ.

So far, at least, he was not suspected of anti-Soviet – or, indeed, anti-Stalin – expression. In fact, so much was Shostakovich the up-and-coming man that he was inundated with commissions, many of them infinitely more absurd in conception than *The Nose*. Shostakovich was an avid football fan – a photograph from the 1940s finds him at a match with friends, shouting lustily at the camera – and a natural choice to write the music for what was intended to be an appropriately modern and appropriately Soviet ballet, something that might preserve Russian pre-eminence in the dance but ease out the tired old bourgeois repertoire on which that reputation had been founded. Originally called *Dynamaida*, then renamed *The Golden Age*, the ballet told the utterly unsurprising story of a Soviet football team's heroic triumph over a pack of bourgeois-fascist hackers and cheats. It was, Shostakovich said, a 'chilly success', and was – in footballing parlance – quietly consigned to the bench.

There were other commissions as well. Shostakovich reacted caustically to the libretto provided for another ballet, originally to be called *The New Machine*. Sarcasm drips off every line of a letter to Sollertinsky:

The theme is extremely relevant. There once was a machine. Then it broke down (problem of material decay). Then it was mended (problem of amortisation) and at the same time they bought a new one. Then

73

everybody dances around the new machine. Apotheosis. This all takes up three acts.

The Bolt, as it was eventually called, was quickly shot down, though it was Shostakovich who was supposed to take the blame for its failure. It had been intended to serve as an allegorical warning to industrial 'wreckers', fifty-three of whom from Donbass, the so-called heart of Russia, had been subjected to one of the first Stalinist show trials in the summer of 1928. Stalin took fulsome revenge, and the 'wild fields' region accordingly suffered disproportionately from his Russification plan and the Holodomor (or 'Terror-Famine') that accompanied it.

A more agreeable subject presented itself to Shostakovich at the end of 1931. That he should in later years have been identified with the morose, introspective, procrastinating Prince of Denmark is doubly ironic given the 'revisionist' nature of Nikolai Akimov's production at the Vakhtangov Theatre, for which Shostakovich composed music. The director reasoned that, in the fast-moving and forward-looking Soviet Union, no one would want to watch some decadent royal agonising over Oedipal urges and the nature of mortality. His solution: fill the stage with swordplay, hunts, and battle scenes; create a spectacular banquet; make the victorious Fortinbras the dramatic heart of the piece. Shostakovich used jazz elements in his score – notably when a drunken Ophelia, cast as a prostitute, sings a cabaret song – but he also took the opportunity to poke fun at 'official' Soviet composers. In one notorious scene, obviously worked out between director and composer,

Hamlet farts through a flute – some remember it being posed jutting from his groin like an erect penis – while the piccolo in the pit orchestra plays an out-of-tune version of a recent 'hit' by Alexander Davidenko written to celebrate Soviet victories on the Chinese border. It's been understood, almost without question, that Shostakovich's music was the best thing about the production, was perhaps too good for it, but more recent research with fuller access to Russian theatrical archives shows that Akimov's appropriation of Shakespeare came closer to the social and political realities of the moment, while Shostako-vich perhaps went in his own increasingly private direction.

There was, of course, more to Akimov's *Hamlet* than a Hollywood-styled confection. The prince, though played as a short, fat comedian, was a kind of revolutionary, showing up the decadence of the court, but also an ambitious fraud, cooking up the story of his father's ghost to ease his own path to the throne. The production, which opened at the Vakh-tangov just a few days before Shostakovich's wedding, was a succès de scandale. Official protests failed to dent its popular-ity, and it did not seem to weaken Shostakovich's position. Akimov was untouchable, though his days were clearly num-bered. For the moment, and particularly with the Association for Contemporary Music being suppressed, music wasn't the main object of government strictures. It was literature, a far more obvious source of subversion, that exercised the authorities. Mayakovsky had been hounded to death; Osip Mandelstam, whose *Kamen* (1913), *Tristia* (1922), and *Stik-hotvoreniya* (1928) had established him as the greatest Russian poet of the century, was banished from Leningrad. A decade after his last book was published, Mandelstam died on his way to a labour camp; a heart attack cheated the authorities of their revenge. Yevgeny Zamyatin, whose novel *We* (1921) had predicted the rise of Stalin, requested to go into exile. He was initially refused but, on the intercession of the writer and activist Maxim Gorky, the regime relented. Zamyatin eventually died in Paris. Gorky had taken the opposite route. The author of *The Lower Depths* (1902) and a brilliant autobiographical trilogy had been in London with Lenin, pointing out 'their' Buckingham Palace and 'their' British Museum, which lent him a certain revolutionary allure. He had lived abroad for long periods, partly for his health, partly as an inveterate nomad, but had always returned home when his country needed him, as in 1914 and again in 1928, when he became the iconic Soviet writer, a staunch defender of what became known as socialist realism.

This, then, was the immediate cultural battleground, but it would not be long before Shostakovich came under scrutiny. His next major project would also have a (loosely) Shakespearean association, and it would be the most remarkable but also the most problematic work of his career so far. For the moment, though, he had found in *Hamlet* and in the figure of the prince a model for his own creative behaviour: disguising his deeper, slower evolution behind a facade of accommodating activity, all the time refusing to be a pipe that others could play on, farting inaudibly under cover of the noise and brouhaha and then denying that the bad smell was his. A worse odour was to follow, though, and with dangerous consequences.

It is perhaps the most famous bad review in musical history. It is also not quite clearly understood. On 28 January 1936, Shostakovich was in Archangel, the latest stop on a tour round Russia. A draft of Symphony No. 4 in C minor was in his brief-case. What he read in that morning's edition of *Pravda* would in due course lead to the shelving of the symphony, but must at the time have made the twenty-nine-year-old composer's blood run cold. The headline ran 'Muddle Instead of Music'. The opera so described, titled *Lady Macbeth of Mtsensk*, was condemned as a 'leftist bedlam' and 'petty bourgeois clown-ing'. Equally damaging, in the coded language of the time, was the charge of formalism, a clear accusation that the work did not address or conform with the principles of socialist realism. The composer 'apparently does not set himself the task of listening to the desires and expectations of the Soviet public. He scrambles sounds to make them interesting to formalist elements who have lost all taste'. The piece also con-tained what could only have been construed as a threat: 'It is a game of clever ingenuity that may end very badly.'

What made the article doubly chilling was that it was unsigned. That usually meant that it had been written or dictated by Stalin himself, though in this case it seems to have been written by a functionary – or a tame journalist – called David Zaslavsky; Shostakovich calls him the 'well-known bastard Zaslavsky' in *Testimony*. Stalin had attended a performance of the opera at the Bolshoi Theatre two days before. Shostakovich had been 'invited' to attend, and did so. He noted to a friend that Stalin had winced at some of the lounder passages but seemed to appreciate the sexual jokes.

However, the leader had risen from his box and left after the third act, and when Shostakovich took a curtain call at the end he was observed to be deathly pale. Stalin's disapproval usually came at a price, and not even public success cancelled it out. What Shostakovich may not have known is that, just over a week before, Stalin had attended a performance of Ivan Dzerzhinsky's *Quiet Flows the Don,* an opera that apparently did accord with the leader's aesthetic requirements.

To compound the irony, Shostakovich had written part of the offending score while once again on holiday in Georgia, but this time in Tbilisi, less than eighty kilometres from Stalin's place of birth. He had been much interrupted, not least by the need to fulfil commissions for the Leningrad Working Youth Theatre and other official companies. He had written music for the play *Rule, Britannia!,* for Kozintsev and Trauberg's film *The New Babylon,* and for a strange revue called *Hypothetically Murdered.* He had, though, pulled out of theatre work and embarked on a new symphony, to be called *From Karl Marx to Our Own Days.* It was later abandoned. Eventually, in December 1932, he finished his opera. During the inevitable delay before its first production, Shostakovich completed other works. His Twenty-Four Preludes for piano were written, seemingly, as daily exercises. If they do represent a kind of musical diary, they offer a disturbing view of the composer's frame of mind at the time. Though written as an orthodox Bachian 'cycle of fifths', they are brief, bitter, and throwaway, and as sarcastic as anything of Prokofiev's. So was the Piano Concerto No. 1 in C minor, written at the same time, in which Shostakovich follows the older composer's example in cocking a snook at the Romantic concertos of Tchaikovsky and Rachmaninoff, with their implicitly 'confessional' manner. As it progresses, though, the work does go deeper. It seems to imply two lines of continuity, one between the expressive extremes of Romanticism and the libertinism of the revolutionary years, and another between that hectic modernity and the intellectual calm and simplicity of purpose of Bach and Joseph Haydn. In its jazzy rhythms, curiously detached viewpoint, and sour opposition of past and present, it has something tonally in common with T. S. Eliot's *The Waste Land*, and it is a similar triumph of ventriloquism.

There is a persistent misconception that Shostakovich's *Lady Macbeth of Mtsensk*, now regarded as one of the great operas of the twentieth century, was a failure and a critical disaster, and that the 'Muddle' review in *Pravda* followed its first performances. On the contrary, the piece was Shostakovich's next great triumph after his First Symphony. It was premiered simultaneously in Moscow and Leningrad in January 1934 and was rapturously received. That may have been the problem. The *Pravda* piece makes much of the work's popular success, hinting that the young composer may only have heard the plaudits and not some serious criticisms. Stalin didn't like to be upstaged; he had eliminated most of his political rivals. How ironic, then, if he lost out in the popularity stakes to a mere music peddler. That the opera had touched a more positive nerve with the public was in no doubt. The piece ran for nearly two years, and its success gave Shostakovich and Nina a measure of domestic security; when they separated briefly in the summer of 1934, economic issues may have played a part

– Nina came, after all, from a prosperous family – and better prospects must have played some part in their reconciliation.

All had seemed well with Shostakovich and his opera until Stalin attended the Bolshoi performance and reached the paranoid (but not necessarily inaccurate) conclusion that the character of the police chief in the third act was a skit on himself – hence his abrupt departure at that point. These scenes were not in the original story, which gives the possibility some added credence. (The story had been inspired by a short novel published in 1865 by Nikolai Leskov, in which Shostakovich saw a powerful allegory of life in pre-revolutionary Russia and a possible first part of what he optimistically conceived as a Wagnerian cycle that would look at the heroic role of women in the liberation of his country. His Narodnik background would have come out in a second opera, about the People's Will revolutionary Sophia Perovskaya, who had organised the assassination of Alexander II; it was never written.)

It is hard, at first glance, to detect the heroic strain in Leskov's heroine, Katerina Ismailova, whose name was used as the title for Shostakovich's later, bowdlerised version of the opera; outside Russia, it is usually known as *Lady Macbeth of Mtsensk*, the title of Leskov's story. The main difference between the original text and the libretto written jointly by Shostakovich and Alexander Preis is the relative sympathy accorded the heroine, which is why the later change of title makes sense – it emphasises her humanity and not her existence as a mere literary 'type'. Katerina is trapped in a loveless marriage to a country merchant, Zinovy, and is bullied by her father-in-law, Boris, whose arrival is heralded by a pompous bassoon melody. In the opening scene, he attacks her for having failed to produce an heir, accuses her of contemplating infidelity, and then, unwisely, reminds her to set out poison for the rats that are gnawing away at their stock.

Zinovy appears to announce that he must go and mend a broken dam – dam-building and the fear of sabotage were powerful signifiers in Soviet Russia – and introduces a new servant, Sergei, who has apparently been dismissed from a previous job for seducing his mistress. Boris demands that Katerina swear an oath of fidelity. So far, the piece has a cheerfully Mozartian contrivance and air of inevitability. There are, however, already signs of cruelty. The servants – who have sarcastically fawned over their master, begging him not to go (dissent by exaggeration?) – now torture Aksinya, one of their number, as if she were a pig fattened for market. Katerina breaks them up, but finds herself grappling with Sergei, which is seen by her father-in-law. Already she seems sensitive, considerate, a flower in the desert rather than an ambitious Lady Macbeth, bored rather than wicked. That is confirmed in the next scene, when she appears at her window and sings with unbearable loneliness 'the colt runs after the filly', comparing her own lot to that of the animals and the birds, who are governed by more natural instincts.

On the pretext of borrowing a book, Sergei seduces her. Boris prowls about below, boasting of his own youthful prowess and clearly considering the possibility of bedding his daughter-in-law, when he discovers that the manservant has beaten him to it. His lust is channelled into sadism as he flogs Sergei. Tired but satisfied, he demands supper. The mushrooms are poisoned. Boris dies just as the priest arrives, accusing Katerina of murder.

The scene ends with the priest wittering about the difference between a man's death and a rat's and quoting Gogol on the perils of mushrooms and cold soups. What follows is the most extraordinary moment in the opera, a huge entr'acte in the form of a passacaglia, signalled by discordant blasts of brass. It arguably represents the most effective orchestral writing yet from Shostakovich, summing up the looming tragedy of the opening scenes.

Sergei turns out to be more potent than Zinovy, but without much stamina or spiritual substance behind his 'educated' exterior. As the huge passacaglia ebbs away, Katerina wants to make love, but her 'Seryozha' merely wants to sleep. They are briefly haunted by a figure they think is Boris's ghost, but it turns out to be the returning Zinovy, who is murdered in turn. Accompanied by one of Shostakovich's grotesque marches, they bury the body in the cellar, the mood darkening with every measure.

On the lovers' wedding day, a drunk man decides to raid the cellar for more booze, and the body is discovered, stinking of decay. The police, irritated that they have not been invited to the celebrations and bored with questioning a hapless nihilist, are galvanised by news of the body's discovery. Katerina and Sergei are arrested and condemned to exile. In one of Shostakovich's extraordinary changes of face, the mood turns from farcical to tragic at the beginning of the fourth act. An old prisoner sings of the long road to Siberian exile in tones that irresistibly recall Mussorgsky. (Perhaps it was just as well that Stalin didn't stay for this scene; in 1933, Siberia was filling up.) Katerina bribes her way into the men's part of the prison but is cruelly rejected by her husband; this inspires a beautiful little arioso lament accompanied by cor anglais.

Sergei has begun to flirt with another convict, Sonyetka, and persuades Katerina to give up her stockings as a gift to the latest object of his affections. Katerina weeps herself to sleep and is roused by the old prisoner just as the sergeant organises the convicts' column for the long walk to Siberia. Spotting Sonyetka standing on a bridge, Katerina grabs her, and the two women plunge into the fast-flowing waters below.

Two murders, promiscuity, a murder-suicide: this is not necessarily the stuff of 'affirmative' Soviet opera. It did, however, strike deep chords with its audience, who would not have missed the vicious satire directed at the old regime and might very well have appreciated Shostakovich's instinctive feminism. He is clearly sympathetic to Katerina and her plight – her lament reappears at a key moment in his highly personal String Quartet No. 8 in C minor – and seems to have treated her murders as legitimate killings. There are, however, other strands to the opera, working at ever deeper levels, not least a palpable nostalgia for the old Russia and its music (some of the convict songs were a legacy from his mother, who remembered them from her journeys in Siberia) and, by extension, its gentler sexual politics.

Shostakovich was drawn to Leskov as one of the few convincing heirs of Gogol (hence the reference), and as an important transitional figure for writers of the Zamyatin generation. *Lady Macbeth of Mtsensk* is an infinitely subtler and grander work than *The Nose*, but its targets and its obsessions are essentially the same, and its tone essentially tragic. That may have appealed to operagoers, but it did not square with official thinking. The word 'formalist' in the *Pravda* review was a hand grenade thrown into Shostakovich's lap. This wasn't the first time it had been used. The previous February, the other important daily journal had complained of formalist elements in the opera, but an article in *Izvestia* did not have the same official force as an unsigned leader in *Pravda*, which is why Shostakovich responded forcefully to the first accusation but largely kept his own counsel over the second. There were other factors too.

In the month that *Lady Macbeth of Mtsensk* was premiered, Stalin announced to the Seventeenth Congress of the All-Union Communist Party, labelled the 'Congress of Victors', that socialism had been achieved. The price of victory was horrific. The first Five-Year Plan had ended some twenty months previously and left the country exhausted. Political purges had liquidated some one million individuals. The Russian countryside was effectively locked down; eight million, and probably more, died as a result of collectivisation. In the summer of 1934, Stalin reorganised and renamed his secret police. OGPU became NKVD; Joint State Political Directorate gave way to People's Commissariat for Internal Affairs. But the techniques didn't change, and neither did the aura of fear. On the first day of December, Stalin's last remaining rival, the hugely popular politician Sergei Kirov, was shot dead in Leningrad. Though Stalin himself, or someone close to him, had undoubtedly sent the young gunman Leonid

Nikolayev, the new police force was able to find some 40,000 'fellow conspirators' and send them off to the camps, while the leader posed mournfully beside the coffin.

This was victory indeed, and it fell to writers and composers to reflect the 'joyfulness' of Soviet life in their work. Optimism was compulsory, pessimism outlawed. Any sense of art as evolutionary struggle was suspended in light of Soviet victory and the triumphant synthesis of Communist ideals. The proletarian organisations that had overseen creative endeavour were disbanded and centralised; the Politburo, or more probably Stalin himself, was the only arbiter of taste. Irony and tragedy, self-conscious modernity, self-serving experiment, were lumped together under a term that surfaced (to Shostakovich's fury) in that *Pravda* editorial. If in 'socialist realism' the regime had found a useful shorthand for all that was good and positive in Soviet art, then in the same way 'formalism' and 'formalist' did service for anything non-approved, from painterly abstraction to reactionary nostalgia in either music or print. Both were broad brushes, or blunt instruments. The distinction was full of logical contradictions, probably better understood in Russia than in the West, but it was never intended to be anything other than an ideological blank cheque to be drawn on as need arose. Novelists were called on to churn out huge affirmative narratives whose only rationale was to underline the viciousness of the ancien régime, the triumph of Bolshevism, and by extension the unassailable goodness and wisdom of the *vozhd*, or leader. Painters and sculptors no longer had to search for subjects: avoid mere pattern-making; celebrate the heroic endeavours of the Soviet worker and soldier, and their sturdy, beautiful helpmeets and children; avoid private gestures; work on the largest scale; understand that Stalin himself is an icon of victory and progress.

Things weren't quite as simple for composers of music. Some key signatures and modes were understood to be 'counter-revolutionary'. Minor keys perhaps suggested defeatism. Too much slow music might suggest that all was not well with the Soviet apotheosis after all. Western importations were simply a new form of 'intervention', conjuring memories of the Civil War, when Bolshevism had to fight former allies for its survival. To some degree, all instrumental music is formalist, autotelic. Unless one imitates natural sounds – birdsong, or the factory hooters Shostakovich brings into his Second Symphony – orchestral and chamber music can have no absolute meaning, or at least none beyond what the composer, his listeners, and his critics choose to impose on it. There is a simple enough solution, one Shostakovich had already tried. Just as artists were encouraged to add appropriate texts where there was any remote possibility of ambiguity, so composers were enjoined to add appropriate titles to their works and to construct song-symphonies that removed all need to interpret the music. All one needed to do was listen to the words.

Whatever Shostakovich meant by his Second and Third Symphonies, he had become a master of ambiguity. The text of *Lady Macbeth of Mtsensk* is subtly inflected, but so too is its score. By contrast, his ballet *The Limpid Stream*, which followed and enjoyed a milder but comparable success, is the blandest propaganda. The paradox is only troubling if both works are lifted out of context. What better response to the suggestion that you are formalist than to write a work of numbing orthodoxy? But why, then, was the ballet criticised alongside the opera in the pages of *Pravda*?

The simple answer was that Shostakovich himself had become suspect, even if individual works could not be condemned on any specific ground. He was treated like a schoolboy who is told that, absence of any evidence notwithstanding, he has a certain look and must be considered guilty of *something*. In February 1936, he was even deserted by friends and colleagues when the Leningrad and Moscow branches of the Composers' Union voted unanimously but probably shame-facedly in support of the *Pravda* article. Among those who ratified its findings was his 'idolater' Ivan Sollertinsky, though Shostakovich probably gave the decision his blessing rather than expose his friend to isolation and possible harm. Another friend, the brilliant critic Boris Asafyev, declared that his own initial enthusiasm had been in error and that the true direction of Soviet opera was, indeed, to be found in Ivan Dzerzhinsky's *Quiet Flows the Don*. Dzerzhinsky's work was adapted from *And Quiet Flows the Don*, a four-volume novel depicting the Don Cossacks during the First World War. With perfect irony, Dzerzhinsky dedicated the piece to Shostakovich, having consulted him during its composition. How embarrassed he must have been to find his work praised by Stalin and to become a runaway success as a result, while his friend and mentor had to stand in a corner. Asafyev also reversed his initial judgement of *The Limpid Stream*, now that was the major work and *Lady Macbeth* the formalist farrago. What part professional jealousy played in all this can only be guessed at (and is often the hidden narrative behind the supposedly ideological contortions of Russian musical life), but it left Shostakovich, for all his precocious fame, dangerously isolated.

He must have recognised, especially after *The Limpid Stream*, that one potential tactic was silence. There was the example of the poet and author Boris Pasternak, who had stopped writing in 1933 rather than write puffs for the regime or risk liquidation by openly criticising it. Exile was also an option. For every artist who had come home to support the revolution, there were others who had left or, like Stravinsky, ostentatiously stayed away. Maxim Gorky had returned to give some theoretical mass to the idea of socialist realism; Zamyatin was in Paris. Shostakovich seemed to prefer a kind of self-imposed internal exile – not the banishment that was handed out to Pasternak for an unguarded moment a little later, but a certain distance and removal.

Shostakovich had largely stayed out of the debates on Soviet symphonism held at the Composers' Union the previous February, doubtless already thinking about his own Fourth (and, if Glikman is to be believed, his Fifth as well). He did not, at first, see fit to change his position on *Lady Macbeth of Mtsensk*, opting neither to defend the work further nor to disown it (though he told one friend that, in the unlikely event of the latter happening, it would be absolute). More importantly, he was not on this occasion required to recant publicly, as he would be a dozen years later. The 'untiring troubadour of Leftist distortion' (as *Pravda* called him) apologised quietly to his colleagues at the Composers' Union for his errors. He did

not disappear, like a million others who had, or like countless others still to come. Stalin seemed to have other plans for
Shostakovich, and they were crueller for being more playful. If
there is a fool, there has to be a king, and it may be that Stalin
took on the role with every bit as much ironic awareness as
the man who had once been tipped to become his court composer. Shostakovich's works were banned from performance
and publication, but he was not completely silenced. The
Fourth Symphony, finished a matter of days before the birth
of his daughter Galina in May 1937, was put into rehearsal
with the Leningrad Philharmonic and only withdrawn when
the composer finally lost patience with the conductor Fritz
Stiedry, who seemed to be making a botch of things. He was
not a poor musician, and so must have been in an agony of
doubt and anxiety, his hand too shaky to sustain the symphony's pounding metres. Rehearsal of a chamber piece could
have been kept secret, but not a work requiring orchestral
forces. So, were the authorities tacitly rehabilitating Shostakovich? Or had the axe simply not yet fallen? Or was the
whole thing part of some larger capricious game? The Kirov
assassination had changed the rules dramatically and instilled
a deep paranoia. Even some of those not arrested as 'conspirators' committed suicide before they heard the knock on
the door, and Shostakovich himself seems to have considered
ending his own life. Deep down, he knew that the smell of
death wasn't going to be limited to the Ismailovs' cellar. Over
the next three years, it would pervade every government cellar
and official basement and would seep into the unconscious of
every thinking Russian.

Four

If 'Muddle Instead of Music' remains one of the most notorious music reviews ever published, the eventual reply is equally infamous. What it means has been debated for seventy years and adduced as evidence for diametrically opposite conclusions. On 21 November 1937, at the Philharmonic Hall in Leningrad, Shostakovich unveiled his Symphony No. 5 in D minor. The score bore the subtitle *Practical Creative Reply of a Soviet Musician to Just Criticism*. The adjectives are worth considering. Did Shostakovich now really accept that the humiliation of early 1936 had been 'just'? Had he now fallen into line as a Soviet composer, alert to the needs of socialist realism and the almost papal infallibility of the *vozhd*? Or was there a sleight-of-hand in the use of 'creative'? Was this seeming recantation merely red-coloured smoke to throw off the watching apparatchiks? There is a further question, by no means an absurd one given Shostakovich's willingness to sign statements he had not written: were the words his at all?

The previous spring, Shostakovich had become an unperson. The *Pravda* article was remembered decades later when Salman Rushdie was made the object of a fatwa for blasphemy against Islam and forced into hiding. The impact on Shostakovich was no less than that, except in his case there was no rush of solidarity from fellow artists and intellectuals. His music was not being played publicly, and – given the paranoia of a society in which a young boy, Pavlik Morozov, could be declared a national hero for betraying his own father to the authorities – it was unlikely to be played privately, either. Old friends and associates crossed the street to avoid him. Merely to be seen with a disapproved person was to risk guilt by association. Shostakovich seems to have drifted into a suicidal lethargy, relieved only partially by a visit to his influential friend and former patron Mikhail Tukhachevsky, a senior marshal in the Soviet Army and a music lover who had access to Stalin. Even though Tukhachevsky seems to have reassured him that the feared midnight knock on the door was not imminent (that fate ultimately awaited the marshal himself), Shostakovich was chronically anxious and utterly alienated.

In that, he was not alone. More than one observer has described the average Soviet citizen's life during the Great Terror as a species of universal solitary confinement. If a child could betray his father, and friends could publicly condemn a once-admired colleague, there were no limits to fear; this is what is meant by totalitarianism. In Shostakovich's case, the visit to Tukhachevsky did at least allow him to start writing music again, playing and improvising with some renewed vigour. Small wonder, though, that the work he produced should itself have been totalising and excessive.

The Fourth Symphony is both a portrait of Shostakovich at his lowest ebb, haunted by a motif that seems to communicate betrayal, and also a portrait of a country where every ordinary cultural parameter was cubistically distorted. The summer of 1936 saw more show trials. Having eliminated the old Bolsheviks, Stalin now set about getting rid of the 'United Centre' (it is the destiny of totalitarian regimes, once they have eliminated enemies to the left and right, to begin an assault on the centre as well, and Stalin liked to pretend that even the middle ground in Russian politics was a potential foe). The head of the NKVD was arrested for falling behind schedule in uncovering counter-revolutionary plots. Half a million were reportedly shot, with millions more deported to Sibera and likely death. The heroes of the hour were the 'shock workers' of the second Five-Year Plan – workers who were lauded for exceeding their quotas. The first and most famous of them all was Aleksei Grigorievich Stakhanov, who on 30 August 1935 mined 102 tons of coal in a single six-hour shift, fourteen times his quota. Others quickly followed: Alexander Busygin in the automobile industry, Maria Vinogradov in textiles, Maria Demchenko in agriculture. The Stakhanovite movement was born. It was, of course, all carefully stage-managed, the flipside of *vranyo* exaggeration-as-satire, and was a defining aspect of the obsessive gigantomania that was characteristic of Soviet life at the time and that Shostakovich 'self-critically' noted in the finale to his withdrawn Fourth Symphony.

His precarious standing with the authorities apart, he had every good reason to have high hopes of the work. The night before Galina was born, Shostakovich and Nina entertained the conductor Otto Klemperer, a great champion of Shostakovich's music in the West who had regularly programmed the First Symphony, along with the First Piano Concerto and the ballet suites from *The Golden Age* and *The Bolt*. A play-through of the new score was arranged on two pianos, and Klemperer was again much impressed. It became a double celebration when Nina gave birth. However, things were proceeding disastrously with rehearsals. Shostakovich's own perfectionism was partly to blame, as he admitted, but it may be that the orchestra was resistant – and few bodies of human beings are more resistant when things aren't going their way than an orchestra. Communication broke down. Apparently on the recommendation of the Philharmonic's director, I. M. Renzin, Shostakovich agreed to cancel the performance. Dangerous rumours had already circulated that the symphony was ridden with formalism. Renzin would not have relished being seen to front such a work by a composer whose reputation was already complex and compromised.

The score was lost during the war – Shostakovich blamed the 'stupid' conductor Alexander Gauk, who seems to have mislaid other manuscripts – and subsequently reconstructed from a two-piano version. In 1961, the Fourth Symphony was performed in Moscow, twenty-five years after its abandonment and two months after the premiere of the Twelfth Symphony before the Twenty-second Congress of the Soviet Communist Party. Shostakovich was unsure that delay had served any useful end, symphonies not being like Chinese eggs that need to be buried in the ground to develop their flavour. By the time it was performed, Shostakovich was a very different composer, and his country had changed out of all recognition. It was still a powerful work, but its creative ecology was no longer the same, and its impact was considerably lessened.

Symphony No. 4 in C minor is immediately and strikingly different from its predecessors. Where they tend to begin quietly and with consideration, the Fourth Symphony opens fortissimo, establishing the blaring intensity it maintains almost all the way through. There is a calculated crudity to some of the figuration, reminiscent of parts of *Lady Macbeth of Mtsensk* and particularly of the priest's music and the police scenes. There is a quieter passage for strings in the opening movement, which, without overt quotation, manages to hint at classical models, but these hints are tattered and almost off-hand, ripped fragments of old scores eddying about in the Soviet whirlwind, almost silenced and lost in Shostakovich's overwrought memory. He had done something similar in the Cello Sonata in D minor, finished exactly a year before he began work on the symphony in September 1935.

The movement oscillates uneasily – as the composer's life and work would – between vast declamatory climaxes and a kind of night music in which muttered ideas and memories are anxiously self-censored. A bassoon theme punctuated by harp chimes seems to conjure up insomnia. The loud subjects will not go away, however, and just when there seems to be a promise of dawn and humane company there is a fresh irruption that some hear as the arrival of the long-feared secret police. It is an exhausting and determinedly ugly movement. Whatever its programmatic meaning, there is no mistaking its technical novelty and boldness. Significantly, the academic Christopher Ballantine devotes more space to it in his *Twentieth Century Symphony* than to any other Shostakovich work. In a chapter headed 'Radical Structural Innovation', he lays out the opening movement's tonal ambiguities, its avoidance of classical development, and its parodic elements (like the sour waltz in C-sharp minor that precedes the complex recapitulation). 'I am not afraid of difficulties', Shostakovich is supposed to have said during the writing of the Fourth Symphony. Whether he meant his present parlous political state or the structural challenges of the new symphony isn't clear, but both can reasonably be assumed. If the Fourth Symphony is thematically disturbing, as a naturalistic portrait of the composer's surroundings and state of mind, it is even more alien in terms of symphonic language. Even so, underneath its roiling surface, there is still something of the language of Haydn and Beethoven, fragmented and embattled but imparting a precarious centripetal gravity to the piece.

The second movement is more explicitly traditional, relying on a Beethoven-like four-note figure and a relatively clear alternation of subjects. It ends, however, with a further echo of the first movement's seeming evocation of the Book of Ezekiel's Valley of Dry Bones, a quietly hellish vision that for all its deceptive calm fails to reassure. The closing movement is as disturbing as the first and even louder. A bleak funeral march is reminiscent of Gustav Mahler. There is, though, no time for mourning. The interment seems to be taking place in the middle of an earthquake. The mourners, if such they be, laugh caustically. Shostakovich briefly seems to lament his loss: hopes, friends, memories, not so much dead and lost as denied and disappeared. The march steadily mounts to a climax of impossible force, some of the loudest music ever written for a conventional orchestra.

Ian MacDonald describes the Fourth as a 'milestone in symphonism'. At the time, it was a millstone. Had the work been performed as planned in 1936, it might have proved the final straw, and Shostakovich might well have joined the long line of the disappeared. On the other hand, its appearance then might have emboldened other symphonic composers in Russia and the West to experiment more dangerously with the form. When it was eventually played, it seemed both a problematic period piece, coloured by what had happened to Shostakovich and to the Soviet Union in the intervening years, and then either ripped out of context or, to take the composer's own analogy, buried in the ground. Certainly, by the time it was performed in the West, its technical boldness stood out but its subtexts and contexts were muted and distorted by subsequent Cold War history.

And yet, how different in tone, manner, and intention is the Fourth Symphony from its successor? The Fifth Symphony, like the Cello Sonata in D minor, is another minor-key work, no less deceptive and hooded, its 'openness' a tactic rather than a sincere gesture, its acceptance by the regime a symptom of wishful thinking on the grandest scale.

The Great Terror continued. Stalin consistently portrayed the revolution as beset by wreckers and counter-revolutionaries on all sides. As the second Five-Year Plan came to an end in April 1937, arrests of army and government officials intensified; even Tukhachevsky fell victim, which must have renewed Shostakovich's anxiety. There were more show trials, again directed at largely imaginary cabals. The 'Right-Trotskyites' included such unlikely bedfellows as former NKVD chief

Genrikh Yagoda (accused of running his labour camps like spas) and the brilliant Nikolai Bukharin, one of the finest Bolshevik minds. The death toll became increasingly abstract as the numbers mounted through the millions.

Shostakovich, though, must have had some modest ground for hope. He continued to work on film and theatre projects and, in spring 1937, was asked to give composition and orchestration classes at the Leningrad Conservatory. A year in purdah may have been deemed sufficient for the moment, but a full-scale rehabilitation still seemed some way off. Working at his alma mater also afforded time for work of his own, rather than official commissions. Between April and July, Shostakovich worked on the score of his Fifth – and perhaps most celebrated – Symphony. Though he continued to produce music for cinema, Shostakovich only wrote one other significant score in 1937. The *Four Pushkin Romances* revived a literary passion of the composer's teenage years. The work carries opus number forty-six, appearing immediately before the Fifth Symphony in his catalogue of works, and the two compositions have a buried connection. Though the *Four Pushkin Romances* were not heard until 1940, Shostakovich used the opening phrase from his setting for one of the poems, significantly called 'Rebirth', as the basis of the great march theme in the symphony. Such self-quotation, common enough among very prolific composers, became an obsession with Shostakovich. What is important here is the text that the phrase introduced: 'So, delusion falls away from my tormented soul, and reveals to me a vision of my former innocence.'

The official Soviet line on the Fifth Symphony was that it represented an artist who had recognised the limitations of individualism and the redundancy of tragedy as a philosophical position and had succeeded through struggle in re-aligning himself with the masses. Whether that was the 'delusion' that Shostakovich felt dropping away, or whether he had simply discovered a way of retaining his 'innocence' – 'purity' might be a more accurate translation – underneath a carapace of conformity remains the issue. A stock comparison casts Shostakovich once again as Hamlet, but a Hamlet who had risen above metaphysical dithering to claim his place in the world. So comfortable a critical shorthand was this that some Russians even today refer to the Fifth as 'the Hamlet symphony'. Beware the pitfalls of metaphor, though. Was this fallen prince of Russian music mad and dissembling sanity, or was he truly out of touch with the world around him? The genius of the music is that it leaves the question unanswerable.

Shostakovich's Symphony No. 5 in D minor was performed at Leningrad's Philharmonic Hall on 21 November 1937. The conductor was Yevgeny Mravinsky, who, along with Kirill Kondrashin, was Shostakovich's favourite. The atmosphere was electric. Though the audience could not have known it, what they heard in the opening movement was a radical simplification of the dense, textural language of the withdrawn Fourth Symphony. Having been damned for formalist complexity, Shostakovich set out from the beginning to demonstrate that he could write with apparent simplicity. Some argue that his model for this was Mahler's Fourth Symphony, which disguises its darker significance behind a child-like directness.

Much of the opening movement is built from a two-note motto, reminiscent of some of the music in *Lady Macbeth of Mtsensk* but a common device throughout Shostakovich's output of the period and even later. The difference here is that what was usually accompaniment is now promoted to main structural device. Like an architect previously criticised for excessive decoration and non-functional ideas, Shostakovich is working with concrete and iron braces. The movement takes on an aspect that resembles Beethoven's Symphony No. 6, the 'pastoral symphony', in which the bucolic landscape is threatened by an encroaching storm. Here, though, the threat is not lightning and rain, but whatever is represented by the stomping of brass and low percussion that seems to cut through the music. If this is really meant to represent Stalin and his gang, Shostakovich was being suicidally brave. The change of atmosphere is palpable. Something has altered radically, and not for the better. The tonal material is soured and rhythmically uncertain. The two-note figure now finds itself in awkward contexts. A pall of fear settles across the remainder of the movement.

The scherzo is precisely that, a broad joke that raises the banality of the first movement into a general principle. Here, it says, is the world in which we now live, all forced merriment and unthinking certainty; they lead, we follow; they say 'Jump!', we ask 'How high?' One instrument or instrumental group follows another, often required to play outside its normal range or character. There is no real question-and-answer, merely an awkward consensus learned by rote. If this is not a sound-portrait of Soviet culture as a tissue of self-serving commands and routine obedience, then it is hard to know what it is.

Shostakovich had made his reputation with the First Symphony, and here again he makes the same dramatic transition from farce to tragedy, from mere cleverness to deeper feelings. However, where the last two movements of the first were pastiche, the remainder of the Fifth was all his own. The largo is unbearably intense, and many among the audience on 21 November 1937 were in tears as it unfolded, thirteen minutes of unmistakable evocation that to the composer represented 'irreparable tragedy' and nothing else. On 12 June, Tukhachevsky had been shot, accused of plotting with Hitler to overthrow the *vozhd*. Shostakovich's slow movement is a memorial to his friend, but also to every other Russian marched away at midnight – the music is quintessentially nocturnal – to a muffled execution.

At this point in the First Symphony, Shostakovich simply intensified the tragic sense. Circumstances had radically changed since then, though. Something very different was called for here. The finale plunges back into the unnatural daylight, the tremulous quality of the slow movement transformed into 'affirmation'. As ever, Shostakovich's structural control and ability to integrate multiple frequencies and apparently unrelated components is uncanny. All the scattered elements of the first movement and scherzo are drawn back in to some of the densest writing of his career. Not even the clashing sound-masses of the Fourth Symphony approach this level of synthesis. And yet the tone is unremittingly ironic. It is as if Shostakovich says 'You demand an apotheosis? *Here* is your apotheosis!' and throws it down defiantly. (He makes clear in *Testimony* that any affirmation to be found in the closing movement is of the hollowest sort.)

As this strange, disturbing music played out, members of the audience in the Philharmonic Hall rose to their feet one by one. The ovation lasted longer than the symphony itself. Mravinsky, who had had problems with Shostakovich over the correct tempi and had resorted to subterfuge to force the composer to make his intentions plain, turned at the podium and raised the score high over his head, as if to say that it was the work and not the performance that should be applauded. Similar scenes played out at the first performance in Moscow the following January, and at a subsequent performance in Leningrad a group of party officials climbed onto the platform and proposed that a telegram of congratulation be sent to Shostakovich from the whole audience.

The unperson had become the People's Artist. Shostakovich's rehabilitation seemed as mystifyingly complete as it was sudden. It was as if all the previous disapproval, the ostracism, and the veiled threat of the *Pravda* editorial were only a rite of passage, a necessarily harsh hazing of the brilliant new recruit, just to see if his mettle ran deep or wouldn't survive departure from the conservatory. The Fifth Symphony quickly became a core work in the Russian orchestral repertoire, played and replayed across the country. In March 1938, the conductor Arturo Toscanini gave the first American performance, in New York, where the reception mirrored a telling division within the American Left. Those who accepted the Popular Front consensus – under which all forms of leftward thought and practice agreed to pull together for a time in the 1930s – hailed the symphony as a representation of the Communist utopia; those left-wing socialists and Trotskyites who had been disillusioned by the show trials and saw the Russian leader as a Red Wizard of Oz, a sly illusionist, were more disposed to find satire and subversion in it.

Not so in the Soviet Union. As Stalin cemented his monolithic hegemony by eliminating the last of the Trotskyite opposition at home, Shostakovich's *yurodivy* gesture seemed to have been taken not so much at face value – since its face value was unmistakably negative – but with an almost mystical transvaluation. From whatever source, word went about that the renegade had created a fine and acceptable work and now seemed to be toeing the line. The famous superscription confirmed it. It was, however, widely known that the words were not the composer's own. Not long before the Moscow premiere, a newspaper reported that *Practical Creative Reply of a Soviet Musician to Just Criticism* was a phrase suggested to Shostakovich by an unidentified journalist. The story went on to say that the composer had 'gratefully' agreed with the words. On such shifting sands are personal mythologies constructed.

Shostakovich was now at least partially insulated by fame. In contrast to the inconsistently translated poets and novelists who had disappeared during the purges, many of them dying behind a barrier of language and unknown to Western audiences, he enjoyed international fame, his music part of the lingua franca of pre-war liberalism. His arrest and liquidation would have sparked an international outcry. As things stood, he was being installed ever more securely in the Soviet cultural establishment. He was confirmed as professor at the Leningrad Conservatory and, in December 1939, elected to the Leningrad City Soviet.

All this called for some reciprocal creative gesture. Shrewdly, Shostakovich announced that his next major project was to be a symphony inspired by Mayakovsky's poem *Vladimir Ilyich Lenin*, ostensibly to be played on Stalin's sixtieth birthday. There could hardly be a creative gesture more politically correct and flattering than to underline the apostolic continuity between the Founding Father and the *vozhd*, and to do it using an officially canonised poet and text. In addition, Shostakovich undertook a new orchestration of the opera *Boris Godunov* by the revered Mussorgsky. It was finished by 1940 but, given the strictures of the time, was fated not to be heard for another twenty years.

The latter project was a labour of love, with its deeply democratic message and its prophetic vision of 'darkness, impenetrable darkness'; the former was as blatant a smokescreen as *From Karl Marx to Our Own Days* had been in 1932. At the very moment Shostakovich seemed to have pulled himself together and wakened to his responsibilities as a People's Artist – as Prokofiev was doing at the same time – his real work took on an increasingly inward and private cast. As deadlines came and went for the largely mythical 'Lenin symphony', Shostakovich turned to chamber music. He even abandoned a projected opera. Two of the three major pieces written before the beginning of the global conflict that in the Soviet Union was known as the 'Great Patriotic War' were for small instrumental groups. There was also a new symphony, but it was as unlike the promised choral work as could be imagined and, again, it laid Shostakovich open to criticism,

As there were between the *Four Pushkin Romances* and the Fifth Symphony, there are clear similarities between Shostakovich's String Quartet No. 1 in C major and his Symphony No. 6 in B minor, the same coded continuity. It was not strictly true that, as Shostakovich claimed, he had not previously written music for string quartet. Some earlier pieces derived from *Lady Macbeth of Mtsensk* material and from *The Golden Age* were found after his death. The form was not widely revered in Russia, where the symphony, opera, and ballet were regarded as the major forms for a classical composer. Shostakovich has next to nothing to say in *Testimony* about the string quartets. And yet, no less than with the fifteen symphonies, Shostakovich transformed Russian perception of the form with the same number of quartets, a cycle that managed to combine epic sweep with penetrating inscape. Perhaps only Bartók's six quartets hold an equal or greater status among twentieth-century representations of the form.

The String Quartet No. 1 in C major was not perhaps the most promising or auspicious start to the sequence. It is almost deliberately backward-looking. Shostakovich tried to minimise its importance by referring to it as a mere exercise, but its autobiographical components – personal grief, idyllic memories of childhood at Irinovka – are hard to miss. And yet, like the symphony that followed, the quartet seems curiously drained of feeling, unlike those intensely confessional quartets by Leoš Janáček, Bedřich Smetana, and Antonín Dvořák that had taken the cue of Beethoven's last great sequence of chamber music and used the string quartet not just as a technical challenge but as an emotional plumb line.

The success of the First Quartet brought Shostakovich an immediate request from the Beethoven Quartet, who had premiered it, for a work they could play alongside the composer himself. The resulting Piano Quintet in G minor won Shostakovich the Stalin Prize. In sequence, it followed his work on *Boris Godunov* and the Sixth Symphony, and it assimilated elements of both within a brilliantly executed classical structure. The Sixth Symphony is another problematic work, the two fast movements hanging like sarcastic appendages from the huge opening slow movement, which is substantially longer than the other two put together. There is some evidence that it attempts to convey Shostakovich's state of mind following the Composers' Union lynching of February 1936. It has the same stillness and plainness that marked the First Quartet, which troubled those critics who required a socialist-realist symphony to spark and fizz. How much that monochrome quality was the result of exhaustion and relief, and how much it followed a deliberate decision to simplify the means is open to question. It has been proposed that the simplicity of the First Quartet was due to the birth of Shostakovich's son, Maxim, in May 1938. The boy's arrival may have set the father thinking again about his own lost childhood, but the notion of Shostakovich writing simple music with one hand while rocking a cradle with the other absurdly misunderstands the absoluteness of his absorption in any musical project, on whatever scale.

The vagaries, negative and positive, of his last two symphonies had left him written out, somewhat as he had been after the first. He was also aware that he was expected to deliver a vast choral symphony, and to some degree the chamber pieces were temporising manoeuvres, written as an excuse for the non-appearance of the 'Lenin symphony'. The Piano Quintet in G minor and the Sixth Symphony also form an important pair in that the same uneasy balance of tragedy and satire is maintained. The leverage is rather different in each case. The symphony tends to hold the two moods in ambivalent opposition, giving the later movements their slightly hysterical cast reminiscent of fairground music. In the quintet, Shostakovich is closer to integrating them. Given that this was a work in which he would also have a hand as performer, with the Beethoven Quartet, its importance is beyond question, and it remains one of the most popular of his chamber works, albeit inconsistently and often inaccurately played.

The Sixth Symphony was premiered in early November 1938. It would attract harsh criticism from the Composers' Union, but only some twenty months later. In *Testimony,* Shostakovich says with palpable relief that it was criticised only 'moderately'. This leaves open a number of questions. Was he simply so inured to criticism that anything short of outright condemnation was a success? Did he have his own doubts about the work? Was the reception, in fact, more positive than is usually supposed by Western observers? To some degree, the issue is irrelevant; by the winter of 1938–9, wider events were in the saddle. The Great Terror had limped to an end, with an inevitable change at the head of the NKVD after

Nikolai Yezhov was discovered to have been plotting Stalin's assassination. His replacement, Lavrenti Beria, a depraved sexual predator whose only loyalties were to Stalin and to his own physical convenience, was to become an icon of Communist decadence. Leon Trotsky's death warrant had long since been signed, and the contract was fulfilled on 20 August 1940 in Mexico. At home, Maxim Litvinov, the commissar for foreign affairs, who had secured US recognition of the Soviet Union in 1934, was replaced by Vyacheslav Molotov in May 1939. As well as lending his (assumed) surname to a favourite guerrilla weapon, Molotov's great achievement was to negotiate, in August of that year, the diabolic accord that 'guaranteed' non-aggression between the Soviet Union and the Nazi government in Berlin. The pact, which sent shivers through Soviet-sympathising 'fellow travellers' worldwide, allowed Germany and Russia to divide Poland between them and Russia to strengthen her Western approaches by invading first Finland and then the three Baltic republics.

In following the Fifth Symphony with a work as introverted and opaquely straightforward as the Sixth, Shostakovich may have invited trouble. As it turned out, by the time his peers gathered to accuse him of recidivism, the Nazi–Soviet pact had been torn up and, for the second time in Shostakovich's lifetime, his country was at war. It was to provide a deceptive respite.

Five

On 22 June 1941, Hitler unleashed Operation Barbarossa on the Soviet Union. The devils' pact was broken. Taking a cue and a codeword from his imagined predecessor, the Holy Roman Emperor Frederick 'Emperor Redbeard' Barbarossa, the Nazi leader set out to conquer the whole of Eastern Russia and the Ukraine and to set the eastern borders of the Third Reich on a line from Archangel on the White Sea to Astrakhan on the Caspian. Early progress was swift. The purging in June 1937 of Shostakovich's friend Marshal Tukhachevsky and some 80,000 other military personnel, including senior strategic cadres, seriously compromised Soviet resistance, adding weight to the suggestion that the Gestapo had been involved in a military plot against Stalin. The Red Army created by Leon Trotsky was still a formidable fighting force but, when deployed across the largest theatre ever seen in modern warfare, its organisational shortcomings were potentially fatal.

The Eastern Front became a byword for brutality. Its long bitter stalemates and sieges – of Stalingrad, most notoriously – were as bloody as any between 1914 and 1918. No one knows how many Russians died during the 'Fascist War' or the 'Great Patriotic War' but – added to the millions shot, starved, and exiled during the Great Terror – the losses might well seem biblical and apocalyptic. However, it is mistaken to think that the war was the greater disaster. Twice as many Russians died at Stalin's hands than at Hitler's, a bitter irony that would in due course be found coded in the conflict's most famous music. On the positive side, though, the war afforded a new sense of national purpose and, for artists and intellectuals who had attracted unwelcome attention from the regime, a certain breathing space. In her oral and textual biography of Shostakovich, Elizabeth Wilson surprisingly heads her chapter on the war years 'A Respite'.

On the face of it, it must have seemed a very tough respite. Leningrad was within reach of the Nazi lightning bolt, sandwiched between Germany's Army Group North formation and the smaller but no less passionate Finnish Army, fired with memories of the November 1939 Soviet invasion of Finland. Winter warfare would prove the undoing of the German Army, but summer conditions eased the crossing of the Dvina and the swift rolling-up of the Baltic republics. By August, Leningrad was under siege. It would last 900 days.

In the summer of 1941, Professor Shostakovich was grading his composition students at the conservatory. He was, however, anxious to serve the motherland, and he applied to enlist in a home defence unit. His extreme myopia unfitted him for active service, but he was accepted as an auxiliary firefighter and began to write musical arrangements – like *The Fearless Regiments Are On The Move* – for performance at the front. The authorities made sure that Shostakovich was seen to be doing his patriotic duty. He was photographed firewatching on the conservatory roof, plying a hose and wearing the helmet that would give him the strange mock-heroic aspect he wore on the cover of *Time* magazine. He also made a morale-boosting broadcast on Radio Leningrad, as did the formerly proscribed poet Anna Akhmatova, whose *Poem Without A Hero* is dedicated to the citizens, living and dead, of Leningrad. She worked on it as the siege took hold, or at least until, like the Shostakovich family, she was evacuated away from the constant bombardment and grinding hunger. The first draft of what was to be her life's work, always referred to by herself and her associates as 'The Poem', was completed in Tashkent in Uzbekistan, but she continued to work on it for another two decades.

Conditions in Leningrad grew increasingly severe as bombing gradually destroyed the city's infrastructure. On 1 October 1941, a week after the composer's frugal thirty-fifth birthday party, Shostakovich, Nina, Galina, and three-year-old Maxim were evacuated to Moscow by aircraft. His mother and his sister Maria remained for the moment in Leningrad but were evacuated the following spring. Given the military situation, with the Wehrmacht and its Panzer divisions in reach of the overcrowded and chaotic capital and with front-line gunfire clearly audible, it was decided the family should move still further east. After a fortnight in Moscow, they boarded a train bound for Sverdlovsk, the industrial and cultural capital of the Ural region. The city had been renamed in 1924 and in honour of the Bolshevik leader Yakov Sverdlov. Prior to that, it had been known as Yekaterinburg, infamous as the final resting place of Tsar Nicholas II and his family, murdered there at the 'House of Special Purpose' on 17 July 1918.

In the event, the Shostakoviches did not get as far as Sverdlovsk. There are poignant stories of the composer standing on the station platform in Leningrad looking sad and distracted, with a sewing machine in one hand and a child's potty in the other, and, later, washing plates in the snow beside the train. Fellow evacuees advised Shostakovich to travel on to Tashkent, where food was plentiful and where many of the conservatory staff and students were already relocated. After a gruelling week on the train, constantly being shunted aside to give priority to troop and hospital transports and relieved only by the company of his composer friend Vissarion Shebalin, Shostakovich decided that the family should disembark in Kuibyshev, on the Volga. This was Russia's war capital, renamed after Politburo member Valerian Kuibyshev, who had died in 1935. Today the city is once again known by its original name, Samara, and its leading tourist attraction is Stalin's strategic bunker, built but never used – composer and *vozhd* were seemingly drawn to one another by some curious magnetism.

The city had proved a refuge in the past. Recently opened in 1940 was the House-Museum of Vladimir Lenin, a second-floor apartment above a merchant's store where the Ulyanov family had lived from 1890 to 1893. Decades later, the Shostakovich family were given rough accommodation in one of the city's schools, before being offered a small flat (with rickety upright piano) at 140 Ulitsa Frunze, where Shostakovich was at least able to work and to draw rations from the commissariat at the Bolshoi Theatre. On 11 March 1942, the family was moved to more spacious accommodation at 2a Ulitsa

Vilonovskaya. By then, Shostakovich was on the brink of his greatest fame, for the premiere of his Seventh Symphony, destined to become one of his most celebrated works, had been given in the city a week previously. The symphony's subsequent history was extraordinary, so much so that an almost mythical reputation has clouded the circumstances of its creation.

It is generally assumed that the Symphony No. 7 in C major, *To the City of Leningrad*, was written in direct response to the suffering of the composer's birthplace during the siege. Shostakovich reinforced this misconception by announcing during his Radio Leningrad broadcast that he was at work on a new symphony, a decision considered heroically optimistic by many of his listeners, given the circumstances of the time. The work was in fact conceived before the Nazi invasion. Anything written in *Testimony* can reasonably be suspected of arrière-pensée, but the claims of that strange, bitter text have to be taken seriously, and in it Shostakovich is clear that the sorrow and the feelings of solidarity he expresses in the Seventh Symphony were for the sufferings of the people of Leningrad not just under several months of Nazi bombardment but under fifteen years of Stalinism. He says, 'It saddens me that people don't always understand what it is about, *yet everything is clear in the music*' (my italics).

'Clear' is either wishful thinking or hindsight at work. However subtly encrypted the symphony's message, and however camouflaged by official propaganda, Shostakovich was still treading a dangerous line. The Sixth Symphony had met with official displeasure for its formalist/individualist elements but had appealed to concert audiences (presumably tired of endless affirmative song-symphonies, like Shebalin's ultra-'proletarian' *Lenin*). Even more dangerous, though, was the kind of reception Shostakovich began to receive after the Fifth Symphony. The audience response to his piano quintet effectively clapped out of countenance the regime's suspicion that chamber music, with its bourgeois, individualistic overtones, was inappropriate in the Communist paradise. It looked for a time as though Shostakovich and his fans were driving cultural policy, not Stalin and the Politburo. A decade after the nadir of his 'Lenin symphony', Shebalin was writing string quartets, as was Nikolai Myaskovsky, while Prokofiev forged ahead with set-aside chamber works.

There was danger as well as benefit in the applause. Shostakovich found himself in the excruciating position of receiving rapturous welcomes from fellow composers whenever he turned up at meetings – this at a time when only one man in the Soviet Union was entitled to a standing ovation. Shostakovich acknowledges the danger in *Testimony* when, in the context of the Seventh Symphony, he mentions how 'intolerable' Stalin found it when anyone else was being spoken about positively. Shostakovich was one of the few Russian composers of any note who had failed to produce a sixtieth birthday eulogy to the 'Wisest of the Wise'. Stalin must, however, have recognised that Shostakovich's propaganda value, increasingly international, outweighed any awkward domestic fame and any habit of ideological error. Since the Red Army's disastrous reverse at Vyazma, the Soviet Union's only urgent priority was keeping Hitler from the gates of Moscow. Besides, Stalin must have felt that he could keep close tabs on his errant composer in Kuibyshev and, if need be, dispose of him. The Volga was deep, and old Samara had always been regarded as the gateway to Siberia.

Shostakovich had begun serious work on the Seventh Symphony in late July 1941. Within a month, he had completed the massive opening movement. He began the second just as the Nazi bombardment began, but despite his Civil Defence duties and the terrifying noise – which later entered the sound-world of his greatest string quartet – he finished it, too, in just two weeks; Shostakovich always had the ability to concentrate in the most distracting of circumstances. On the day he made his Radio Leningrad broadcast, he played through the finished parts to a group of friends. He did the same when he arrived in Moscow, at the home of the composer Aram Khachaturian, whose First Symphony had been on the same programme as Shostakovich's Fifth at its premiere.

The half-finished score and the manuscript of *Lady Macbeth of Mtsensk* were among the few personal possessions Shostakovich took with him from Leningrad. He resumed work on the symphony in Kuibyshev, which must have given a homesick inflection to its inscription, and finished the score two days after Christmas 1941. There were immediate plans to put the new work into rehearsal. Mravinsky and the Leningrad Philharmonic had been evacuated to Novosibirsk, which would have presented severe logistical problems, so, on 5 March 1942, in Kuibyshev, Samuel Samosud conducted the first performance with the Bolshoi Theatre Orchestra. It was met with huge acclaim. Copies of the score were smuggled out of the Soviet Union on microfilm. Arturo Toscanini conducted the Seventh Symphony at Radio City Music Hall. A month before, on 22 June, Henry Wood, who founded the Proms in London, gave the first British performance, which was attended by this writer's father, an experience he remembered for the rest of his life. A short-wave radio fanatic, he remembered with even greater clarity and passion hearing the Seventh Symphony broadcast from Russia. On 29 March 1942, Grigory Stolyarov had given the second performance, in Moscow, during an air raid. The event was transmitted worldwide. The 'Leningrad symphony', as it was universally known, became a powerful symbol of wartime resistance, though Shostakovich regretted that it was celebrated less for its music than for what he called 'tangential matters'.

Of all the performances it received, none was more important symbolically and (to Shostakovich) emotionally than one in the city that had inspired the work. It is perhaps the only time in musical history that military operations were coordinated on such a scale to assist an orchestral concert. In what was known as Operation Squall, Leningrad's military commander launched a bombardment of German positions designed to quieten the guns long enough for the work to unfold uninterrupted – a detail that makes occasional intrusions by mobile phones and winter coughs at concerts seem absurdly trivial. It is probably also the only known occasion when recruitment posters called not for soldiers to serve the motherland but for musicians. The score had been flown in on a medical transport, but there was no active orchestra left in Leningrad, and certainly not one large enough to perform a work that required huge forces equivalent to the massed sound of the Fourth Symphony. The Philharmonic was far to the East, and the surviving members of the Radio Orchestra – not many more than a dozen out of the original hundred or so – were in a parlous condition, riddled with hunger and dysentery, like everyone else in the city. The conductor Karl Eliasberg (who seems to have dropped the second half of his German-sounding name for a time, choosing to be known as Karl Elias) was so ill that he collapsed while walking home from rehearsals. In an echo of what had happened to Shostakovich during the hunger years of the Civil War, he was granted extra rations and a bed at the Philharmonic Hall. The orchestra players, too, were given food from a fast-dwindling supply.

Even so, it was a motley orchestra – a collection of old men, musically literate infantrymen plucked from the front line, and a few professionals – who gave the *Leningrad* its apotheosis on 9 August. Not even the first performance of Olivier Messiaen's *Quartet for the End of Time* in a German Stalag on broken instruments and in front of an audience of several thousand (that is the version of legend; the instruments were almost certainly sound, if rudimentary, and those attending at Gorlitz probably numbered no more than a few hundred) has such a powerful emotional resonance. Even so, it wasn't the *1812 Overture* that the authorities had hoped for.

The Seventh Symphony is scored for a very large orchestra, with heavily reinforced brasses and percussion. Though his later comments seem to contradict it, Shostakovich gave a programme note that relates the Seventh quite explicitly to the war.

'Allegretto – Suddenly war breaks into our peaceful lives.' Perhaps the most famous passage in the whole of Shostakovich's music, and the most celebrated of his marches, is signalled by a half-heard side drum whose tattoo cuts across the almost bucolic opening, played by strings and winds, bassoons predominating, leading to a beautiful violin melody. The march rises to a shocking crescendo, with percussion and extra brasses adding to the onslaught. The juggernaut passes, leaving flutes, violins, and a surviving bassoon from the opening pages to stagger, disoriented, towards the climax. There is, however, hope in this, some determination to keep alive the music of the opening. Violins and flute rework that same material, transforming it into something celebratory that manages to defy the ever-present martial threat.

'Moderato (poco allegretto) – Memories.' If this looks back to the past as the programme suggests, it is here where Shostakovich may make the most explicit connection between the Leningrad-that-Stalin-destroyed and the city-that-Hitler-merely-finished-off. The opening melody is far from nostalgic. It has a restless quality, developed by second violins that are soon joined by low strings and woodwinds. There then comes a bizarre waltz, its wild eroticism a reference perhaps to the days of total sexual licence after the revolution. Another march cuts across it, before the movement ends in an oddly chastened spirit.

'Adagio – Our country's wide vistas.' This is the heart of the symphony, according to Shostakovich. It begins with a plain wind theme underpinned by harp, which is Russian to its core. Having established his landscape, Shostakovich then peoples it in an intense string melody that gradually draws in strings and harp again. There is a storm, but whether it is natural or man-made isn't clear, though the latter is hinted at by a quiet side drum. Shostakovich seems to be saying that Russia has weathered adversity and invasion for much of its history, an endless cycle signalled by the repeated and transformed opening material that comes back in soft woodwinds and plucked strings at the end, with a tam-tam suggesting the country's beating heart.

'Allegro non troppo – Victory and a beautiful life in the future.' The finale is played attacca, without a break, opening with muted strings and a faint roll of thunder in the distance. Vernacular voices call back and forth on horns and oboes, but there is intense purpose in this closing movement as well – trumpets and strings in rugged solidarity. Their determination simply grows, in apparent obedience to some relentless historical logic that beats away underneath. The logic of its C-major tonality, the classical key of affirmation, becomes clear at the end as percussion joins in with what sounds less like a victory celebration than some ritual of rededication. The Seventh Symphony lasts one hour and a quarter but seems to touch on a far longer cycle of history.

The backlash was quick and powerful, in the West at least. In a matter of eighteen months, the 'Leningrad symphony' had supplanted Jean Sibelius's Second Symphony (a surprise choice, but one confirmed by pre-war ballots) as the favourite of American concertgoers. Once the euphoria of those early performances had worn off, and the dramatic context was forgotten, American critics began to condemn Shostakovich's

Seventh Symphony as a work of propaganda, overblown and rhetorical. By the end of the war, and for many years thereafter, it was performed rarely in America and only somewhat more often in the United Kingdom. In Russia, the situation was different. The weak-minded composer Tikhon Khrennikov railed against Shostakovich, enraged that his supposed rival should have seen fit to criticise his opera *Into the Storm*, a feeble retread of Dzerzhinsky's *Quiet Flows the Don*. Though mutual criticism had long been part of the collegial identity of Russian composers, given and received disinterestedly, Khrennikov was outraged. As soon as Russia rid herself of the hated Allies – only minimal pretence of mutual friendship while the Führer was still to be defeated – she would crush Shostakovich like a bug under a fingernail.

Perversely, though, Shostakovich seemed bent on engineering the backlash. The so-called Honoured Artist of the Russian Soviet Federative Socialist Republic (RSFSR) might have seemed immune to criticism after the international triumph of the Seventh Symphony. Its successor, though, was to be one of his most problematic works. Recognised now as one of his greatest achievements, the Eighth Symphony disappeared from the Western concert repertoire immediately after the war, like its predecessor, and never received more than a lukewarm reception in the Soviet Union. Why did Shostakovich write an optimistic symphony at the start of the war and a tragic one at its end? However, during the cultural if not political thaw of the 1960s, the Eighth Symphony assumed a new significance in the West, which it has borne until very recently, when again its perceived shortcomings have assumed priority.

The end of 1942 saw Shostakovich again seriously ill, this time with gastric typhoid. He spent some time in a sanatorium near Moscow, able to work on nothing more substantial than the Piano Sonata No. 2 in B minor, a bitter, enervated work that again foregrounds Shostakovich's satiric side. He had also, the day after writing the final cadences of the Seventh Symphony, begun work on a third opera, *The Gamblers*, which was never finished but was apparently written in a similar sarcastic spirit. Shostakovich had languished in Kuibyshev, and he planned to travel to Novosibirsk to be with Mravinsky and his friend Sollertinsky, but Shebalin, now the new director of the Moscow Conservatory, offered him a chair in composition. In April 1943, Shostakovich and Nina returned to the capital.

The children, for the moment, remained by the Volga. Though danger was ever-present, Russian fortunes in the war had turned. 'General Winter' had proved to be the decisive commander. The siege of Leningrad was eased, though more than half a million of the city's inhabitants had died of starvation, and the suffering would continue for another year. On 2 February, the siege at Stalingrad ended with German surrender, and the Soviet Union began to counter-attack. In July, just as Shostakovich was beginning the Eighth Symphony, Russian and German armour clashed at Kursk in an almost medieval joust that altered the course of the Eastern Front. It was the greatest tank battle in history. By the time the Eighth Symphony was premiered in Moscow, the Allied leaders – Winston Churchill, Franklin D. Roosevelt, Stalin – were preparing to meet in Tehran, this two years before the more celebrated Yalta conference, to discuss the disposition of the post-war world.

The Symphony No. 8 in C minor was written in just ten weeks, between 1 July and 9 September 1943, and largely at the new Composers' House at Ivanovo. For some critics, the speed of composition is reflected in a drastic loss of technical – or possibly emotional – control. MacDonald suggests that Shostakovich 'blew a fuse' and produced an 'earthbound' work lacking the 'vital electricity' that set him apart from almost all of his contemporaries. While acknowledging that something was happening to the composer and that the work does significantly diverge from his usual approach, such comments smack of what another observer, the critic Christopher Norris, calls 'ideological reaction'. They are also deeply coloured by a very particular brand of hindsight. Works can only very carefully be judged by what came after, though the illusion that they can be explained by what went before is almost as pernicious.

As gramophone recordings became increasingly important in the post-war period, interpretations of Shostakovich's work were increasingly coloured by performance values and by the vagaries of interpretation. Successive conductors took sizeable liberties with the composer's expressive and rhythmic markings. Recordings of the Eighth Symphony are wildly variable in duration. The composer's son, the conductor Maxim Shostakovich, turned it into a dark personal odyssey and stretched the symphony out to some seventy minutes. Semyon Bychkov's version with the Berlin Philharmonic reduces the work to a sequence of bleakly nihilistic fragments and slows the first and last movement unbearably. Bernard Haitink seems to have intuited the work's tightly organised symphonic argument, and he brings it in at around the one-hour mark, an astonishing variation. Only the trusted Mravinsky, who had visited Shostakovich at Ivanovo during the writing of the piece and may have influenced the upbeat allegretto finale with his enthusiasm for the first four movements, seems able to balance dramatic and structural values and to produce a recording both emotionally satisfying and faithful to Shostakovich's intentions.

Because the Eighth Symphony exists as a complex of antagonistic interpretations, it can be difficult to describe neutrally. Certain details are incontestable. The work is dominated by a huge adagio opening movement, which is twice the length of the finale and four times as long as movements two and three. However, the architectural balance of the piece is achieved by playing the last three movements without a break, a device Shostakovich returned to in his Ninth Symphony and string quartets.

The adagio begins in the home key of C minor, a tonality that might recall the 'fate' motto of Beethoven's Third Symphony or Schubert's Fourth (titled *Tragic*). The lower strings establish a strong dotted phrase that gives the work a deceptively vehement beginning and perhaps suggests that it begins in medias res, as if the symphonies from the Fifth onwards really were part of an epic cycle. This gives way to a softer theme, immediately reminiscent of the opening movement of the Fifth Symphony. Shostakovich instructed that the strings bow *sul tasto*, or above the fingerboard, a device that bleaches the sound-colour considerably. There is a throat-clearing interlude for the lower woodwinds before the second subject gets under way. Violins play robustly over a steady string pulse with violas and cor anglais emphasising a sanguine and apparently optimistic mood.

With a return to the nervous opening figure, the flutes suggest that all is not as it seems. A militaristic drum beat establishes a note of urgency, though the basic pulse remains constant. There is an abrupt, powerful climax that completes the dynamic gamut from a near-inaudible *pppp* at the start of the violin melody to a stunning *ffff* as the central conflict breaks. Suddenly up a gear, the woodwinds bleat ominously, while, at some distance from the main action, the horns and cellos sound distant warnings of disaster. A heavy-footed march follows, and it is hard not to picture the trumpets and glockenspiels of Nazi bands at Nuremberg. This 'bloated and unfocused mess' ends with a plaintive cor anglais solo that MacDonald, not in any way disposed to hear the virtues of the Eighth, considers 'interminable'. The end of the adagio is no longer than necessary and says no more than it needs to.

The second movement is a scherzo with a surprisingly dour aspect. It recalls Shostakovich's more obviously satirical writing, but it seems to have moved a step beyond merely guying fascist goose-steps to launch a more general attack on extremism of thought and the failure of intellectual generosity. The composer makes considerable use of widely spaced woodwind pitches over a basic D-flat tonality that is determinedly unsymphonic and banal in character.

It is almost certain that the sound effects and battering ostinatos of the E-minor third movement are intended to suggest military conflict. There are shell bursts, machine-gun fire, panicky musters, and urgent high-pitched trumpet calls, but again the onomatopoeic character of the music always seems prepared to be drawn up into something larger. In place of juxtaposition, Shostakovich allows the dissonant conclusion to dissolve into the succeeding largo, which represents the heart of the closing meta-movement. It is cast as a passacaglia, a set of polyphonic variations over a ground bass, similar in form to the great interlude in *Lady Macbeth of Mtsensk*. Stage by stage, the music is transformed from bleak defeatism (every phrase abruptly shut off or wearily attenuated) to a level of philosophical confidence that is too guarded and carefully mediated to be characterised as optimism.

The ending is unexpectedly affirmative. It opens with a parping bassoon melody that sets in motion a sequence of languid philosophical discussions drawing in violins, a flute, cellos, and oboes. There are quotations from earlier movements and from other works, notably the Piano Quintet in G minor, with its betrayal motif. It has become customary to hear the conclusion as devoid of animation, but it sounds more like the gesture of a composer who has already completed his argument and just spends a moment or two listening to it circulating, not quite reliably, round its orchestral 'audience'.

The radicalism of the Eighth Symphony is that it is a meditation on the whole idea of symphonism. MacDonald suggests that it 'swings a sandbag against the listener's skull', but it is in many ways the least histrionic of the wartime symphonies and a return to the modernist experiment of the equally unloved Fourth Symphony. There is far less inscape, far less newsreel, far less sound-tracking and special pleading than in its predecessors, and yet, when simply experienced rather than interrogated under ideological premises, it tells far more about war, intolerance, and suffering than almost anything else Shostakovich wrote.

Whether it was less about the war years than about the pre-war sufferings of the Russian people, as Shostakovich suggested in *Testimony*, is difficult to judge in hindsight. But certainly its apparently tragic tone was sharply at odds with the mood of national optimism that followed the improvement in military fortunes. Shostakovich was entirely aware of this. About a month after the premiere, Shostakovich wrote to Glikman, telling him that a Composers' Union meeting to discuss the work had been cancelled because he was unwell, but that he looked forward to the criticisms of his colleagues, which would surely – as they had with the Fifth Symphony – spur him to greater creativity: 'Instead of one step backwards, I will make one step forwards.' The letter drips with sarcasm.

A guide to the emotional world of the Eighth Symphony can be found in the Piano Trio No. 2 in E minor, which is ostensibly a memorial to his friend Sollertinsky, who died in early 1944 as the piece was being written. Its eerie opening, with false harmonics on the cello articulated against a dead bass from the piano, captures a mood with unnerving precision. The pace picks up rapidly but with no sense of resolution, and the scherzo, when it comes, is as sardonically playful as anything Shostakovich wrote, violent and only relieved by what the author David Fanning identified as the 'emotional shock absorber' of the slow movement. Shostakovich's ability to juxtapose comedy and tragedy, a wild galop against a funeral march, is one of the consistent but most opaque aspects of his work. Which mood is the dominant one? When there is no clear resolution, what are we to conclude?

The authorities tried to pass the Eighth Symphony off as a memorial to the dead of Stalingrad, thus justifying its sombre character by turning it into 'Shostakovich's Requiem'; he uses the analogy himself in *Testimony*, of the Seventh and Eighth Symphonies together, but with a sharply different emphasis. It was harder to find a rationalisation for the Ninth Symphony's apparent refusal to celebrate victory in the Great Patriotic War. As he had done before, Shostakovich told the press he was working on just such a piece, but in *Testimony* he commented bitterly that 'they wanted a fanfare from me, an ode … and they demanded that Shostakovich use quadruple winds, choir and soloists to hail the leader. All the more because Stalin found the number nine auspicious'. Shostakovich had another reason for considering it in the opposite light. Were he to end *his* Ninth Symphony with a vast apotheosis, it would invite unsupportable comparison with the great 'choral symphony', Beethoven's Symphony No. 9 in D minor. Stalin might be satisfied with the comparison; Shostakovich's fellow composers would use it to mock him. It may also be that, having written upbeat wartime pieces and undemanding fodder for the NKVD Music and Dance Ensemble [*sic*!], and having collaborated with Khachaturian on *The Song of the Red Army* for the national anthem competition, he considered his patriotic duty done for the present.

The desire for privacy, the need to claw back some personal space for private meditation, had been sharpened by grief.

Sollertinsky, perhaps his greatest friend, died suddenly in February 1944. The hope that they might work happily together in Moscow evaporated in a moment. Shostakovich poured his sadness into the Piano Trio No. 2 in E minor, a work that begins in unbearable desolation and ends in a brutal danse macabre as Shostakovich and all Russians watched the unfolding horror of the Nazi death camps, progressively 'liberated' as the German line rolled backwards. He may have wanted private space, but for Shostakovich history always pushed at the door. That is also unexpectedly true of his String Quartet No. 2 in A major, also finished in 1944, shortly after Galina and Maxim were returned to the family in Moscow. It is the absolute opposite of its predecessor: massive, dark, almost symphonic, and full of satire, just like the Ninth Symphony.

Stalin had wanted an apotheosis. Shostakovich gave him 'just music', as he wryly commented of the Ninth Symphony, but it is music that encodes some of his fiercest and most damaging caricatures of the leader. The music is full of brutal lockstep figures, which by now always seem to herald the arrival of the *vozhd*, and sharp-eared listeners will detect a curious Wagnerian tinge, apparently a reference to the kinship-in-hell of the two dictators who between them had just accounted for some twenty-five or thirty million lost souls. The Symphony No. 9 in E-flat major is not Shostakovich's greatest work, but it is not the slight and baffling trifle that is sometimes suggested. Shostakovich knew what he was in for long before the premiere. The now familiar two-piano reduction had given the Composers' Union time to sharpen its collective knives. The respite was over.

Six

Shostakovich wrote very little music in 1946. There is no need to look around for any midlife crisis or stylistic quietus. There was enough in his and the world's recent experience to provide a convincing correlative and reason for relative silence. He may have been approaching his fortieth birthday, but he was tired and weakened by disease, and, after the bruising encounters of the previous ten years, his natural instinct was to retreat. The family spent the summer at Komarovo, outside Leningrad. In subsequent years, they occupied apartments in a dacha owned by Nina's father. They decided not to move back permanently to Leningrad itself, though Shostakovich's mother and sister did. Though he continued as a professor in the conservatory, Shostakovich also had a post in Moscow, and at the beginning of 1947 the Shostakoviches moved into a new flat in the capital.

There were more pressing objective reasons for his silence than academic duties and family upheaval. The end of the war laid a pall of ambiguity over the Soviet Union. Former allies were already declared enemies. Members of the Red Army unfortunate enough to have been captured were brought home – many against their will – and immediately liqui-dated. Any contact with the West was considered a dangerous contagion, 'curable' only by liquidation or exile in the Gulag. Given such a drastic transvaluation, even writers and composers eager to mollify the regime could not know what position to take or what literary sources to employ. The discovery that a certain Russian writer was admired in the West would be enough to guarantee their proscription and an uncertain fate for anyone aligned with them. Shostakovich found himself in this position when he wrote soundtrack music (only the second significant score of 1946) for Grigori Kozintsev and Leonid Trauberg's film *Simple People*, only to find the film condemned as 'un-Soviet, antipatriotic and anti-People'. In such an atmosphere, the song-symphonies dried up and opera stalled; only once-suspect chamber music and instrumental works were considered safe, simply because they had no text that might be misinterpreted as counter-revolutionary.

Shostakovich's String Quartet No. 3 in F major was largely finished at Komarovo, and it seems to have cost its creator dear. The man who could produce vast orchestral scores at lightning speed and work in almost any conditions, oblivious to surrounding noise, struggled to complete it. There was nothing new in the structure. Indeed, the trajectory of the quartet is identical to that of the Seventh Symphony and the other wartime works, with a peaceful, almost folksy opening cut across by a sardonic scherzo, then plunged into what can only be interpreted as grief (another powerful passacaglia) before ending ambiguously. It is thought that the slow movement, worked on while Shostakovich visited his mother, bears marks of his distress at Leningrad's shattered cityscape.

The quartet's unmissable numerological code – two against

three, Stalin against the people – is again familiar from previous works. And, again, Shostakovich provided the work with a programme note that attempted to pass it off as a simple memory of the late war, and the ambiguity of the last movement as a moral and philosophical question: why? Even here, though, his real intentions were not far from the surface. Were the 'rumblings of unrest and anticipation' in the opening movement really just pre-war fears and nerves (Stalin had apparently ignored warnings of an impending Nazi attack) or did they point to something more subversive?

There were rustlings of unrest inside the Soviet monolith and suicidal uprisings in the Gulag, and the deep destructive rumble that would haunt the later twentieth century was heard for the first time, down in the basses, as the Soviet Union embarked on her own nuclear programme. In August 1949, the first viable Soviet nuclear weapon, based on the Nagasaki bomb and constructed with the help of leaked American documents, was secretly detonated in Kazakhstan – but Shostakovich had already anticipated his country's search for a 'superweapon' and its apocalyptic possibilities. The Iron Curtain described by Churchill at Fulton, Missouri, in March 1946 had long since thundered shut, and in Stalin's mind the Cold War had already begun. In a sense, it had begun its modern phase during the interventionist stage of the Civil War, when Bolshevism was assailed from all sides by former Russian allies, but most historians possessed of a long view understood that the Russian bear had been a fearsome figure for centuries – at least since the time of Peter the Great, or even that of Ivan the Terrible, almost two centuries earlier still.

While Americans searched inventively for 'Reds under the beds' and Communists in the State Department, the Soviet regime began smoking out formalists again. Socialist realism was back in the saddle and every bit as capricious and amorphous as it had been before. There was a Humpty Dumpty logic to the term: it meant exactly what Stalin said it meant, or, in more practical terms, what his cultural enforcer said it meant. Russia was entering 'the Time of Zhdanov', or *Zhdanovshchina*. The new cultural commissar, Andrei Zhdanov, was a former party boss in Leningrad, and thus already familiar to Shostakovich. A hoodlum whose viciousness increased sharply in the presence of beauty and intelligence, Zhdanov pulled off the extraordinary historical trick of making Senator Joseph McCarthy look like Solomon, and the rabid editor of the Nazi tabloid *Der Stürmer*, Julius Streicher, like Savonarola.

Not only was Zhdanov a philistine, he was an anti-Semite as well. The cultural paranoia of *Zhdanovshchina* seemed to have breathed in the poisonous smoke of the Holocaust. Much as Hitler had done in *Mein Kampf* with respect to the Western Front in the First World War, Stalin began to see the Jews behind Russia's wartime reverses in the Second World War. He and Zhdanov made the same equation of Jewish people and modernism, the latter being only another, deceivingly positive term for formalism. Anti-Semitism in Russia is a subject that requires more extensive discussion – that it was endemic, there is no doubt; that it touched even respectable members of society, otherwise liberal in attitude, cannot be ignored. That Shostakovich was aware of it through his liberal parents but remained soft on it in earlier years is also unfortunately true, though he makes clear in *Testimony* that he later regretted this and refused to join in anti-Semitic jokes. Much of his work of the post-war period was to be suffused with Jewish themes.

Shostakovich seems at first to have been relatively sanguine, or at least fatalistic, about the latest clampdown. 'I had gone through it at a younger age and the subsequent storms and bad weather had hardened me', he suggests in *Testimony*. After the Eighth and Ninth Symphonies, the *yurodivy* mask must have seemed full of holes, but perhaps experience had simply given Shostakovich another layer of skin. There are other reasons he could afford to be philosophical. He hadn't written much music in 1946. If there were no new scores, there was nothing to criticise; at the same time, there was less pressure to turn out affirmative propaganda works. By the spring of 1947, Shostakovich's non-musical workload had also risen. In addition to his teaching responsibilities, which called for regular travel between the capital and the 'hero city' of Leningrad, he was appointed chair of the Leningrad Composers' Union – irony of ironies, in view of what had happened there and what was just about to. Not for the first or last time, Shostakovich seemed to be cornered into the role of poacher-turned-gamekeeper, fronting the very organisation that had more than once decried his work as anti-revolutionary and bourgeois. A short time afterward, in the summer of 1947, Shostakovich was appointed a deputy to the Supreme Soviet of the USSR, an essentially meaningless role that mostly involved passing on edicts from Stalin and the Central Committee, but again a time-consuming one; even rubber-stamping has certain unavoidable protocols. Perhaps the government was playing its version of the *yurodivy* game: identify the trouble-maker, but instead of punishing him, make him part of the system and keep watch that way instead. Also, the more files and directives Shostakovich had to read and initial, the fewer 'dissident' works he might write.

There was one further reason why Shostakovich might initially have regarded Zhdanov's reign with some equanimity. It was clear that, again, literature was the primary target. The regime reserved its harshest criticism for Boris Pasternak, who had embarked on *Doctor Zhivago* in secret, and for the poet Anna Akhmatova, a revered figure whose collection *Anno Domini MCMXXI* had been published the year Shostakovich began writing music seriously, but whose great *Requiem* was not published in Russia until 1987. Akhmatova had been criticised and excluded before, but her reputation remained untarnished. In May 1944, she gave a reading in Moscow at which there was a spontaneous ovation; Stalin, who claimed sole right to such acclaim, was convinced that it had been organised. Akhmatova became an early target of Zhdanov's as a result. In August 1946, she and Mikhail Zoshchenko, author of *The Poker* and the autobiographical *Before Sunrise*, were humiliatingly expelled from the Writers' Union and 'unpersoned'. In contrast to Akhmatova – and to the stoical Shostakovich when he had been criticised at the height of the Great Terror – Zoshchenko was emotionally destroyed, reportedly begging friends to speak to him or even acknowledge his presence. (Akhmatova did later write the pro-Stalin cycle of poems *Glory to Peace* in the hope of having her son freed from the Gulag, but the Great Leader was unforgiving.)

Shostakovich watched sympathetically. He must have been relieved when Zhdanov's next target was the cinema. Soviet film had iconic standing both at home, as a symbol of revolutionary progress away from the old bourgeois art forms, and abroad, as an example of a radical art form developing its own new visual poetry. Nothing more thoroughly damned directors such as Vsevolod Pudovkin and even the great Sergei Eisenstein (for whose *Alexander Nevsky* Prokofiev had written a brilliant score) than that they were admired in America, Britain, and France. It was, however, only a matter of time before Zhdanov's attention turned to the art form he understood least of all, and therefore most thoroughly suspected of unsoundness.

In the interim, science was his next target, leading to the Laputan nonsense of Lysenkoism in genetics, which was merely pseudoscientific Stalinism. But, in January 1948, the inevitable happened. Zhdanov chaired the First Congress of the Composers' Union in Moscow. It had all the hallmarks of a witch-hunt, but, as always, with some elements of comedy theatre. Delegates laughed uproariously and self-consciously at Zhdanov's 'jokes' and applied themselves with a will to the prearranged consensus. The ostensible target of criticism was the Georgian composer Vano Muradeli, whose opera *The Great Friendship* was found to be infected with formalism (read: it had annoyed Stalin). Called to give an account of himself, Muradeli gave the astonishing – and doubtless scripted – reply that Khachaturian, Myaskovsky, Prokofiev, and Shostakovich were all to blame for his work, because as the directorate of the Composers' Union they had turned formalism into an orthodoxy that was hard to resist. The 'Big Four' were subsequently removed from their posts in the directorate and replaced by nonentities. Criticism was extended to include Shebalin and Gavriil Popov. As the assembly gave way to absurdity, it looked as if all classical music might be declared redundant. In his closing comment at the first session, Shostakovich simply made a plea for freedom of expression and fatalistically waited for judgement to be handed down. He didn't have long to wait. The following day, he had to listen to the chair describe his music as sounding like a pneumatic drill or a *dushegubka*, the latter a particularly chilling comparison since it refers to the vans specially adapted by the Nazis to function as mobile gas chambers. Having heard his work dismissed as a kind of hyper-naturalistic musique concrète, Shostakovich simply thanked Comrade Zhdanov for a speech that would provide everyone with food for thought. It was an insincere vote of thanks from a condemned man, grating with sarcasm.

The absurdities of *Zhdanovshchina* were to appear – or rather to be shrewdly concealed – in Shostakovich's secret cantata *Rayok*; some members of his circle claim to have seen or heard drafts of it in 1948, but it was probably written almost a decade later. In the event, Zhadnov would not be around much longer to haunt Shostakovich in person. At the end of August 1948, he fell ill and was unable to demonstrate his visionary grasp of soil science and agronomy at the Soviet Congress of Agricultural Sciences. On the final day of the month, Zhdanov died. He had been a heavy drinker for some time, but there were suggestions that he had been poisoned. That idea was first mooted in 1953 during the so-called Doctors' Plot, a series of claims that predominantly Jewish doctors – supposedly conspiring to assassinate Soviet leaders – were routinely injecting their patients with syphilis and cancerous cells. This was, unsurprisingly, a paranoid fiction cooked up by the MGB, the latest incarnation of the secret police, to justify another round of anti-Semitic terror during Stalin's last days. It has since been suggested that Stalin himself was behind Zhdanov's assassination. The leader had been capable of shedding crocodile tears over Kirov's funeral bier and wouldn't have hesitated to hasten the effects of Zhdanov's compromised liver once the trusted commissar started to become too big for his boots. The later Soviet leader Nikita Khrushchev describes in his memoir Stalin angrily warning Zhdanov about the perils of alcoholism. It was family advice, because the *vozhd*'s daughter, Svetlana Alliluyeva, had married Zhadnov's son, Yuri – but the show of concern might have been a good cover, because Stalin was known to be enraged by Yuri's criticisms of Lysenkoism.

Unfortunately for Shostakovich, Zhdanov's death merely brought to the fore a new tormentor. The composer Khrennikov was a passionate and apparently sincere believer in the principles of socialist realism, though in the later *glasnost* days he claimed to have spoken and acted only as he did because of threats to his family. His Second Symphony, of 1943, was an earnest expression of, as the composer put it, 'the irresistible will to defeat the Fascist foe' and contained no individualist ambiguities whatsoever. At the end of the war, Khrennikov had served with the Red Army music corps and was in Berlin when the war ended. He joined the Communist party in 1947 and was a deputy in the Supreme Soviet. He became secretary general of the Composers' Union during the purge that ousted the 'Big Four' and held the post until the Soviet Union came to an end. Driven by envy and spite (evident in his fury that the Seventh Symphony should have been likened to Comrade Beethoven's work), Khrennikov hounded Shostakovich and Prokofiev with particular fury and took a special delight in declaring their work unfit for performance and ordering that all recordings should be destroyed and scores pulped. In *Testimony*, Shostakovich recalls being called in to the Composers' Union to receive yet another dressing down from Khrennikov, the Salieri to his Mozart. He apparently snarled at a secretary for interrupting their closed-door discussion, only to discover that it was Stalin on the phone. So discomfited was Khrennikov that he conducted a long conversation with the leader without ushering its subject into an ante-room. Shostakovich closely studied a portrait of Tchaikovsky while his fate was discussed behind him. Shostakovich's hatred – and his penchant for scatology – was evident when he put about the story (probably untrue) that Khrennikov had been so nervous while presenting a list of Stalin Prize nominees to the Great Leader – bearing in mind that nobody could tell, day to day, which names were acceptable and which would damn a supporter to the farthest reaches of the Gulag – that he had lost control of his bowels.

Shostakovich was not only once again unpersoned but his

work was also airbrushed out of Russian musical history. The weeks after the congress were awful. Following Zhdanov's formal announcement on 10 February, Shostakovich was forced to undergo a period of self-criticism and apology for what Khrennikov had called the 'frantically gloomy and neurotic' nature of his symphonies. The writer Pasternak was disgusted that Shostakovich (and Prokofiev, who wrote a letter of recantation) should not choose the path of silence, or else leave Russia and work more freely elsewhere, but exile was never an option for Shostakovich. Outsiders, including Western critics, have been rather affectedly 'mystified' and disappointed that, once again, Shostakovich should have been at least outwardly willing to toe the line. What they cannot understand, though Pasternak should have, is the reality of Stalinist 'criticism'. Gangs of street children were organised to throw stones through the Shostakoviches' windows (Maxim remembers trying to repel an attacker with a catapult) while shouting the regime's stock insult. One thinks of Harrow schoolboys throwing stones at dachshunds in 1914, when anything German was suddenly anathema, but what did Muscovite street urchins understand by 'formalist' other than a sanctioned opportunity for misbehaviour?

Shostakovich's troubles were not limited to sticks and stones. In September 1948, he was dismissed from all his teaching posts for 'professional incompetence', though, in a perfect illustration of the regime's capriciousness, he was immediately appointed a People's Artist of the RSFSR – another meaningless title. Stalin seemed inclined to keep Shostakovich close while holding him down. The strings were pulled at will. Shostakovich was told that his cantata *Poem of the Motherland*, written to mark the thirtieth anniversary of the Bolshevik Revolution, was 'inadequate' (it probably was), but Stalin personally approved his film music for Alexander Dovzhenko's *Michurin* and Grigori Aleksandrov's *Encounter at the Elbe*, two exceptions to an almost total Zhdanovist clampdown on film-making in 1948.

Shostakovich was grateful for the income. Within eighteen months, he would resume giving recitals in order to make ends meet. By then, though, he would have visited the United States as a delegate of the very men, Stalin and Khrennikov, who had declared his work unperformable at home. Shostakovich resisted the trip, pleading airsickness and poor health but secretly dismayed by being asked to live out a lie: 'It was humiliating for me to take part in a spectacle like that. I was a formalist, a representative of an anti-national direction in music. My music was banned and now I was supposed to go and say that everything was fine.' After being sent abroad to eat American breakfasts and play for frivolously dressed Americans at Madison Square Garden – a piano reduction of the scherzo from the Fifth Symphony, in front of what he genuinely believed would be his last audience of any size – he had to go home and listen to the campaign against formalism wind itself up with fresh denunciation of 'rootless cosmopolitans'. If the target was Stravinsky, the formalist who had just returned from behind enemy lines was sure to be caught in the crossfire. The term barely needed decoding any more.

Much has been said about the 'Jewish' content of Shostakovich's Violin Concerto No. 1 in A minor. It was in fact one of a series of works that seemed to defy the edict by showing that Jewishness was, in fact, deeply rooted in Russian soil. Shostakovich admired the 'laughter through tears' aspect of Jewish music: 'I never tire of delighting in it, it's multifaceted, it can appear to be happy while it is tragic.' Though this is transparently a reference to his own method, too, it is important to keep his gestures of solidarity with the Jewish people in focus, given that he inhabited a culture in which anti-Semitism was effectively pro forma – and hard to avoid – by omission, if not commission. He said in *Testimony* that he often judged a person by their attitude to Jews and felt that any person with 'pretensions of decency' (an odd way to put it, but that may be a lapse of translation) could not be anti-Semitic, a prejudice that, he had learned from childhood, was a 'shameful superstition' deeply ingrained in Russian culture. Elsewhere, he seems to suggest that speaking of Jews with a mocking laugh was taken among sophisticated people to be a sign of confident sangfroid. To a large extent, the oppressed Jew seems to have stood as a symbol for Shostakovich himself. He was careful not to release his Jewish-inspired works at the time. The austere song cycle *From Jewish Folk Poetry*, with its themes of privation and stoical survival, was not heard until 1955, some eight years after it was written, by which time Stalin was of course dead. The same applied to the String Quartet No. 4 in D major. This was the last of the 'Jewish' works, and again seems to follow the same dramatic logic of the wartime symphonies, beginning in folkish simplicity before its humane melodies are overpowered by snarling dissonances and further reminders of the Stalin motif.

The most important and self-revealing work of the sequence, though, is the Violin Concerto No. 1 in A minor. Written for the brilliant conductor David Oistrakh, who made a speciality of the Beethoven concerto, it is a work again palpably haunted and nocturnal. Western critics and those who have happily swallowed the official representation of the war symphonies have accepted that this first violin concerto is Shostakovich's response to the Holocaust. The fate of Europe's Jews and Gypsies was clearly on his mind at this period – prompting memories of his father's love for Gypsy songs, perhaps – but the concerto is also deeply and demonstrably autobiographical.

The opening movement again captures the atmosphere of sleepless anxiety Shostakovich felt during the Great Terror. The opening nocturne has the colourless, drained quality of the pre-dawn, but the daytime world that replaces it in the following scherzo is clownish and strangely pompous, a perfect aural recall of the back-stabbing and obsessive eagerness-to-please of *Zhdanovshchina*. Sitting at the heart of all this is a figure who would shortly reappear in the Tenth Symphony – not quite the movement's protagonist, certainly not its still centre, but possibly its unquiet one: a motif consisting of the notes D–E-flat–C–B. In German notation, this effectively spells out D–S–C–H, unmistakably the composer's own signature. This is the *yurodivy* at his most masked and ironic, but also inscribing a flagrant graffito.

The third movement is another emotional passacaglia, a fresh outpouring of emotion for the dead of the Great Terror and the war. It reappears in the closing movement, but this time unexpectedly transformed. Shostakovich was about to embark on the finale when he was forced to make his recantation to the Composers' Union. The closing sequence, marked 'Allegro con brio' as if in bright optimism, is characterised as a burlesque and cast in two-note (Stalin), three-note (the people), and four-note (Shostakovich) cells, a grisly dance of death that sees the two individuals – composer and *vozhd* – gradually give way to the masses. This time, though, there is a question mark. Shostakovich's lifelong faith in the people seems to be at its lowest ebb.

Seven

The poorly disguised distaste with which America welcomed an ailing, nervous Shostakovich to the Waldorf Astoria peace conference in 1949 was a perfect expression of free-world complacency. The journalists, writers, and fellow musicians who met Shostakovich could not possibly have known what he had suffered over the last dozen years. What they saw was a man who seemed to represent the polar opposite of liberal individualism and self-determination, a man for whom art was a form of ideological ventriloquism. How ironic that at home Shostakovich should have been condemned for embodying the former and failing to live up to the latter.

Just as the wartime hero seemed to have feet of clay, the wartime ally was also undergoing a radical transformation in Western demonology. The Soviet Union, like America born in revolution, was now part of a vast Manichean drama, an alternative history. Some weeks before Shostakovich received his infamous phone call from Stalin, the tabloid *Komsomolskaya Pravda* announced that Alexander Mozhaysky had engineered the first powered flight in a heavier-than-air craft in 1884, a generation before the Wright brothers. Later in 1949, the Soviet Union demonstrated that it might not have been the first nation to explode an atomic bomb but it was not far behind, in what quickly became an apocalyptic technological and strategic contest that brought the world close to disaster. It was already working hard to put a Soviet citizen into orbit and to claim the upper atmosphere for Communism.

The Great Terror seemed to have come round again. There were fresh purges, as Lavrenti Beria and Georgy Malenkov weeded out the last remnants of the Zhdanov circle, and new show trials, which now extended to what was becoming known as the 'Soviet bloc'. Most notorious of them was the 'confession' under torture of the Hungarian cardinal József Mindszenty, who was found guilty of treason and other offences and sentenced to life imprisonment. It was only the first of many such trials in Eastern Europe. Thousands of Russian political prisoners coming to the end of their sentences were deemed not to have made sufficient restitution and were simply rearrested as 'repeaters'. There were revolts in the Gulag during 1950 and 1951, which were taken as 'objective' confirmation that the repression had been justified in the first place and put down with brutal satisfaction.

The déjà vu effect was underlined by a return of the old revolutionary gigantomania. In October 1948, the *vozhd* had unveiled the Great Stalinist Plan for Remaking Nature, a project to transform the Siberian climate permanently by planting huge forests. It was abandoned five years into its span, when the Russian King Canute breathed his last. It did, however, provide Shostakovich with a subject that pleased even Khrennikov. On his return to the Soviet Union, Shostakovich had been expected to produce a major work like the Fifth Symphony, or possibly one of the abandoned Marx- or

Lenin-inspired works to redeem his reputation. Shostako-vich's oratorio *Song of the Forests* was orthodox enough to win him a Stalin Prize and the much-needed stipend of 100,000 roubles that came with it. He also wrote acceptable music for films such as *The Fall of Berlin*, but the real Shostakovich can be gleaned from his next numbered opus. Dedicated to the memory of his friend Pyotr Vilyams, the String Quartet No. 4 in D major was the work of a man embittered, anxious, angry, fearful, all understandably so – but also stoically defiant and, as ever, utterly absorbed in the making of music.

His personal sorrows were far from over. One does not nec-essarily hear his distress in the main work that occupied him in 1950, but in private Shostakovich began to drink vodka in larger amounts, a habit that perhaps explains the odd mixture of neglect and almost smothering affection he displayed to Galina and Maxim. This morbid distortion of the paternal instinct became even more evident after Nina's death, when the children were essentially left in the care of a housekeeper but subject to maudlin displays of emotion when their father was around.

Shostakovich was awarded a dacha in Bolshevo as a reward for having taken part in the peace congress, but he never seems to have settled there, preferring for the time being the Varzar apartments in Komarovo and, increasingly, a spe-cially reserved cottage in the Composers' House created by the Composers' Union in Repino. Indeed, in 1961 he handed back the Bolshevo house and bought a new one in Zhuko-vka – an odd gesture, since he would have been entitled to sell the former and use its proceeds to fund the purchase of the latter. The Shostakovich children eventually inherited the Komarovo home.

Despite the profound suspicions of the authorities, Shostakovich was sent abroad as a delegate to further peace conferences, travelling to Warsaw in the spring of 1950 and to Berlin just before Christmas 1952. He also headed Soviet delegations to music festivals in East Germany, notably the Bach bicentenary celebrations in July 1950. Shostakovich had returned to playing by this time, and on the same trip he also performed in Berlin a piano version of one of Bach's Concertos for Three Harpsichords. More important personally, though, was hearing the pianist Tatiana Nikolayeva playing Bach in Leipzig. Her pianism was an immediate inspiration to him, and on returning home Shostakovich began work on his own Twenty-Four Preludes and Fugues, Op. 87.

It is a very different work to the earlier Twenty-Four Preludes, Op. 34, which had been written as daily exercises while the wrangles over *Lady Macbeth of Mtsensk* continued. The later sequence has little of its predecessor's air of musing privacy, and it is significant that, though he did later make a recording, Shostakovich did not play the cycle in public. He did, however, have to present the work to his masters for their approval or constructive 'criticism'. He began work on the Twenty-Four Preludes and Fugues in October 1950 and worked hard on the score at the Composers' House at Ruza, completing the work in February. In May, he submitted to what had become a routine discipline: playing the work over two nights to a small audience of stone-faced party officials at the Composers' Union. As he played, they scribbled on their notepads.

At the end of the performance, Shostakovich came forward – looking exhausted – to explain the work's genesis. His remarks were the now-familiar mixture of self-denial, diffidence, and defiance. He told his jury that he had 'always found it quite hard to compose, and therefore, so as to make it easier for me perhaps, I too have to practise this sort of scribbling'. He explained that he had been influenced by Bach (still a safe bet), and by the reassuring thought that even the master needed this kind of exercise to keep his technique honed. Nevertheless, the work seemed to write itself, and still seemed so fresh that he found it difficult to offer any personal judgement of it. On an earlier occasion, pressed by Stalin himself to explain the genesis of his work, he struggled to make himself understood and fell back wearily on 'inspiration'. All his life, though, Shostakovich had put hard work over any such mystical visitation.

It might be thought that his comments amounted to an admission of formalism in the conventional sense, or it may be that once again Shostakovich was throwing up neutral-coloured smoke to hide his real feelings. On party instructions, he was at this time receiving home lessons in Marxist political economy and was learning to dull their boredom with acts of exaggerated self-abasement: 'I am a worm compared to His Excellency.' The first listeners were unambiguous in their opinions. One Sergei Skrebkov, then a secretary at the Composers' Union, immediately pounced on the absence of any reflection of 'Soviet reality' and damned the work as ugly. One of his old tormentors, Vladimir Zakharov, director of the Pyatnitsky Choir, who had denounced all classical music at the infamous Zhdanov meeting and been rewarded with a secretarial position for his correct thinking, warned Shostakovich that he should not slip back into old mistakes. Zakharov had said in *Pravda* that the Eighth Symphony was not music at all, 'just' a composition, and that it had nothing at all to say to the people.

There were defenders at the meetings, notably the composer Georgy Sviridov and the pianists Maria Yudina and Nikolayeva. The latter premiered the work in Leningrad just before, and again just after, Christmas 1952, but it was Yudina who spoke up for the need to have music with 'inner content' as well as music that simply reflected contemporary reality. She also defended the work's occasional moments of satire. What, in this world, could be wrong with that?

Surprisingly, one looks in vain for any deeply coded significance in the Twenty-Four Preludes and Fugues. Shostakovich told his first audience that he thought of the piece as not a unified cycle but a series of exercises, and it is hard to avoid that impression. The middle and final fugues are magnificent, but there is a faintly academic air to the pieces, interspersed with claustrophobic melancholy, which suggests that Shostakovich really was trying to write his way out of a blocked or fallow period.

It may have worked. Within a year, Shostakovich had written a tough, muscular new string quartet, a piece that seems to allude in every movement to his own past, but with a new defiance and perhaps with a sense that things were at last about to change. Its great sequel, the Tenth Symphony, would be one of his greatest and would emerge in that new

– albeit chastened and still anxious – world that the quartet seems to promise. In the meantime, though, he continued to make a living as a performer, touring the Baltic republics and the Transcaucasus and writing the occasional rather routine score, including a cantata, *The Sun Shines Over Our Motherland*, again to words by one of the regime's most reliable poets, Yevgeny Dolmatovsky, who had written the words for Shostakovich's entry to the wartime national anthem competition. The only other significant work of 1951 was *Ten Choral Poems on Revolutionary Texts*, though he returned to more agreeable – even nostalgic – material at the beginning of the following year with the *Four Monologues on Verses by Pushkin*.

There is a multiple irony in Yudina's remark. For a time in 1952, it seemed that the regime agreed with her. In April, *Pravda* announced that satire was dead in Russia and that the country needed a new Gogol to poke a little constructive fun at the 'shortcomings' in Soviet society. As ever, it was difficult to interpret what this meant, beyond the fact that an opinion expressed in *Pravda* was assumed to have the status of an instruction. If satire was 'dead', that meant contemporary iterations were unpleasing and all must strive harder. Given that the socialist paradise was a matter of official fiat, and that the right-wing anarchist Gogol was not a name normally bandied about in the official press, this should have sounded warning bells. The very few Russian writers who took up the challenge were immediately arrested and charged with 'unpatriotic libel'. Pasternak was in the final stages of *Doctor Zhivago*, but was probably by now so case-hardened – his mistress, Olga Ivinskaya, had just been deported to the

Gulag – that he would not have taken the bait. Those who did were mostly obscure and their work forgotten.

The *Pravda* editorial was a honeytrap. It would be another year before there were real signs of thaw. In November 1953, *Pravda* announced a more realistic attitude to socialist realism. In response, Khachaturian published a short article that called for modest freedom of expression for composers. The following month, the literary magazine *Novy Mir* published an essay called 'On Sincerity in Literature' by Vladimir Pomerantsev, which suggested that realism in fiction should be judged according to actual empirical standards rather than abstract ideals. It looked as though a thaw might be coming. Like Pasternak, though, Shostakovich kept his thoughts to himself. He was wise to, for a year later *Novy Mir's* editor was dismissed for having published the Pomerantsev article. The delay is significant, reflecting not so much immediate retribution for an ideological lapse as a further brutal about-turn. It was the falsest of springs.

A second audition of the Twenty-Four Preludes and Fugues had been called in the summer of 1952 by the Committee for the Arts, and this time the work, so thoroughly calumniated mere months before, was praised to the skies. That effectively cleared it for public performance, and Nikolayeva set about learning the score. Her work with Shostakovich in this period yields a fascinating insight that the composer had begun work on his Tenth Symphony long before the date normally assumed. It is clear from the whole course of Shostakovich's career that his major works – and the symphonies in particular – all had a long, slow gestation and were often intermingled in his mind with smaller-scale works. The very fact that he was contemplating another symphonic work at all was a sign of some optimism, but something of that was already evident in the String Quartet No. 5 in B-flat major.

This remarkable piece was written in under two months, between 7 September and 1 November 1952. Its predecessor had still not been publicly performed, and the stirrings of the Tenth Symphony must have been uppermost in Shostakovich's mind. Nevertheless, he forged ahead with the work, and it is one of his finest in the form. The opening seems innocuous enough, but it is soon packed with extraordinary dissonances and contentions between the violins and the other two strings. There are references to *Lady Macbeth of Mtsensk* (still possibly the work he most treasured) here and in the slow movement, and references, too, in bewildering profusion to the symphonies of the Great Terror and war years. The climax of the work is anything but unambiguously affirmative, but there is light and movement in the Fifth Quartet – a new, stronger, and possibly shrewder creative identity. Underneath it all, but this time so utterly transformed that it is seldom commented upon, is the four-note D–S–C–H motif that was to become the almost obsessive signature of the Tenth Symphony.

When asked by Volkov what that work was about, Shostakovich said plainly that its subject was Stalin and Russia in the Stalin years, but pointed out that nobody seemed to have recognised this 'yet'. To some extent, he had been dealing with the same subject in every major work for the last two decades, but with the Tenth Symphony that subject matter could come to the fore with new force and clarity – not least because, by the time it was first performed, The Greatest Genius of All Centuries and All Nations was no longer around to hear it, let alone issue an opinion. The unintended comedy of Stalin's passing is now well known and has even been the subject of a feature film. It wasn't quite as funny at the time.

Between March 1953 and November 1955, three of the people who had made the greatest impact on Shostakovich left him and the world. The early months of 1955 saw the eventual premiere of *From Jewish Folk Poetry*, which Shostakovich had suppressed during the time of institutionalised anti-Semitism. He also completed soundtrack music for *The Gadfly*, a flowing Tchaikovskian score that has remained perhaps the best-loved of his occasional works. For the rest of the year, though, he composed little and spent much of his time at Komarovo, nursing his seventy-seven-year-old mother. Having survived both a violent mugging twenty-one years earlier and the rigours of wartime Leningrad, Sofiya Kokoulina died on 9 November.

If hers was an expected loss, that of Nina the year before had been shockingly sudden. A trained physicist, she had been working on cosmic radiation at a maximum-security installation in Armenia when she fell ill and was discovered to have terminal cancer of the bowel. The couple had been living apart for some time – Nina was having an affair, or at least an intense emotional friendship, with her colleague Artem Alikhanian, while Shostakovich was involved with his brilliant composition student Galina Ustvolskaya – but when Shostakovich heard the news he immediately flew to be at her bedside. She died shortly afterwards and was brought back to Moscow for burial. It was under a cloud of grief that the widower played the piano part in *From Jewish Folk Poetry* at its premiere five weeks later. (There is but a single reference to Nina in *Testimony*, where he points out that *Lady Macbeth of Mtsensk* was dedicated to his future wife; one wonders which woman mattered more to him.)

Those personal losses apart, it should have been a time of fresh optimism and renewed energy for Shostakovich. The greatest single obstacle to his life and happiness had been removed some time previously. In his final years, Stalin grew increasingly paranoid. Plots against him – most of them imaginary – proliferated. He spent most of his last months behind the wire fences, booby traps, and mines that surrounded his dacha. After the Nineteenth Congress in October 1952, he had reorganised the party once again, preparing for yet another mass purge. The struggle for succession began, clandestinely and in an atmosphere of deep dread. On 5 March 1953, Stalin slowly choked to death as the result of a cerebral haemorrhage, apparently haunted by visions that played out on his sickroom ceiling. He had lain unattended for some time, those around him too fearful to approach the soiled and stertorously breathing remains of the man who had been proclaimed the greatest and wisest ruler of all times, but whom they also knew to be one of history's most pitiless mass murderers. His son Vasily reeled around drunkenly, while doctors tried desperately to avoid making any kind of fateful decision about the leader's treatment and party officials muttered in corners. On the very same day as Stalin's passing, Prokofiev died in Moscow and was denied his full obituary as ordinary Russians went into a bizarre spasm of grief, not yet ready to accept that Stalin was truly gone and that the killing years might finally be at an end. In fact, the killing did not end until Stalin was safely bricked up in the Kremlin Wall Necropolis. Many in the hysterical crowds that gathered to file past his coffin were crushed by tanks. It was both a legacy and a dark prophecy.

Eight

The Symphony No. 10 in E minor is one of Shostakovich's very greatest works. In the wake of Stalin's death, he retreated once again to Komarovo and resumed work on a score that, according to Nikolayeva, had obsessed him for some time. The harsh lockstep that marched across earlier symphonies seems to have gone, though its influence can still be felt. Instead, the huge opening movement centres on a steady thematic progress built out of throbbing short figures from the low strings, with more extended lines coming from the violins and violas. The clarinet signals a new idea and direction, in which the material builds and builds to an almost unbearable climax. And this is only the first movement, which enters a vortex of emotion unparalleled in his work hitherto. In Shostakovich's numerology, this points to the Russian people, suddenly but ambiguously released from the tyrant's grip. There is a mechanical quality to the opening measures that gradually relaxes as the movement gains momentum. As an aural representation of the coming Khrushchev Thaw, it is near perfect. It is also virtuosic symphonic writing. Soviet listeners chose to hear traditional folk material in its melodic content; anyone listening now cannot help but be struck by its daring modernity.

The terrible weight of the past reasserts itself in the middle of the movement. The ghost of Stalin can be heard yelling its familiar two-note figure, and the scherzo that follows is almost entirely dominated by the Georgian gopak metre, which had come to stand for the tyrant in Shostakovich's work. So far, so very similar to the implicit drama of previous symphonies, though never before had Shostakovich laid out his theme in quite such a complex manner. Stalin makes an unmistakable appearance in the second movement march, with a military drum stoking up fear. The third movement is a waltz, three-quarter time being one of the ways Shostakovich alludes to the common people. But his own signature is there: D–S–C–H again, introduced by woodwinds – but also, less expectedly, the name of one of his pupils, Elmira Nazirova, given as E–A–E–D–A. The allegretto third movement is more mysterious, at least until the now-familiar D–S–C–H motif comes to the fore, interspersed with horn clarions that some have traced back to Mahler. Implicit here is a certain retreat from history, an absorption in the self and in music of great inwardness. The movement also refers obliquely to a central motif in *Lady Macbeth of Mtsensk*, a treasured work, which Shostakovich would shortly revise. There is a hint of warning, as if to say, 'Stalin may be gone, I may be moving from the spotlight, but things will go on much as before, only secretly.' Like all conscious Russians, Shostakovich must have been aware that to be relieved of Stalin only to fall into the bloodied hands of Beria – the former secret policeman was now locked in a power struggle with Malenkov and Molotov – was a very ambiguous fate indeed.

There is a curious air of farewell about the Tenth Symphony. Given that his Fourth had still not been performed, Shostakovich may well have regarded this as a de facto Ninth – which has been since Beethoven an almost mystical number for a writer of symphonies. Mahler was haunted by it and did not live to see his Ninth Symphony performed. He also failed to complete his Tenth, which might help explain some of the Mahlerian references in Shostakovich's work. He himself was haunted by the possibility that he had nothing more to write, likening himself, in one letter, to Gioachino Rossini, who had written his last work at the age of forty and then lived on for his full biblical span without putting down another note. (He might also have mentioned Sibelius, then still alive, but also silent for nearly thirty years.)

The block that afflicted Shostakovich after the Tenth Symphony can be attributed to many things: Nina's death; his mother's; the inevitable rough handling the work received at the Composers' Union. Above all, though, it is a reflection of the enormous effort that went into its writing. The Tenth Symphony is a masterpiece of compression, allusiveness, and control. It also finishes with the only real and unambiguous apotheosis he had hitherto felt able to write. It is brief enough, but all the more significant for that. The second subject of the third movement and the great finale that celebrates – or, more realistically, looks forward to – the liberation of the Russian people are both liberally inscribed with the D–S–C–H motif, which sounds increasingly defiant and self-confident. 'It is not yet over,' the music seems to say, 'but there is a way through the darkness.'

The Tenth Symphony was premiered under Mravinsky on 17 December 1953. It is a mark of the uncertainty under which everyone had lived since the death of Stalin that there was no immediate or outright criticism, but it was determined that the work should be subject to proper scrutiny. A week later, Beria was executed (begging for his life, according to one universally enjoyed version, and killed in a firefight, according to the more likely one). The following March, the Tenth Symphony came before the Composers' Union. True to form, Khrennikov excoriated it. Dzerzhinsky, whom Shostakovich had helped with his *Quiet Flows the Don*, was another of the attackers. The familiar consensus was that the work was individualistic and failed to reflect the realities of Soviet life. In a devastatingly simple and effective ploy – the *yurodivy* again – Shostakovich admitted that he'd made mistakes: the first movement was too long and the others disproportionately short. Significantly, he said nothing about its content.

The last three months of 1953 had seen a flurry of Shostakovich premieres: the Fifth Quartet, then the Fourth, then the Tenth Symphony. The spring of 1954, however, saw little activity. The beginning of the year saw the first performance of the delightful Concertino in A minor for two pianos, which Shostakovich wrote for Maxim, who was studying at the Moscow Conservatory and was bent on a performing career. Shostakovich later wrote the Piano Concerto No. 2 in F major for his son as well, but Maxim eventually settled on conducting instead. Galina, meanwhile, seemed to have more of her mother's scientific genes, and she enrolled as a student of biology at Moscow University. Maxim and Galina – now sixteen and eighteen, respectively – must have been alarmed by their father's depression, though they were by this time used to his absences and utter absorption in music; he and Maxim at least had that in common. What they thought when Shostakovich remarried just eighteen months after Nina's death isn't reliably recorded, but friends were appalled. Margarita Kainova seems to have been a totally different personality to Shostakovich's vivacious and cultured first wife, and the attraction seems to have been based entirely on her physical resemblance to Nina. They had met at the World Festival of Youth, where Shostakovich was judging yet another 'massed song' competition and Kainova was working for Komsomol, the Communist youth organisation. He engineered an introduction through the musicologist and RAPM founder Lev Lebedinsky. It was an uneasy union, based on no apparent common interest, and in 1959 Shostakovich divorced Margarita, leaving Maxim to remove her from the Moscow flat.

If Shostakovich's private life was disastrous, his public career proceeded cautiously and, in some respects, rather strangely. He continued with some occasional film work. This is of some immediate relevance because his next major work was to be criticised (on aesthetic rather than ideological grounds) for being 'cinematic'; some even suggested that listening to the Eleventh Symphony was a bit like experiencing an epic film minus the images. He had scored Mikheil Chiaureli's *The Unforgettable Year 1919* in 1951, but he made his finest contribution to the form in 1964, when he wrote music for Kozintsev's 1964 film *Hamlet*, a version of the play that significantly restored the political dimension largely missing from Laurence Olivier's classic 1948 screen version. When *Hamlet* was shown in the West, the *New York Times* said that Shostakovich's music was 'splendid and stirring'. He later cannibalised music from a 1932 stage production of *Hamlet* for Kozintsev's 1971 film *King Lear*. The two Shakespeare plays remained close to his heart. Almost the only music he wrote in 1954 was the Festive Overture in A major, to mark the thirty-seventh anniversary of the Bolshevik Revolution. While it is clear that an air of tragedy would not be fitting in such a work, it is an extraordinary score in that it almost entirely lacks the mordant irony one expects to find in Shostakovich. More disturbingly, that same referential quality – full of quotes, allusions, secret codes, and mise-en-abyme effects – seems to be entirely lacking even from a much more personal work, the String Quartet No. 6 in G major, which marked his return to canonical forms. It is also largely missing from the Eleventh Symphony, Shostakovich's first genuine critical success in the form since his Seventh – it won him the Lenin Prize – and a work very much concerned with the principle of recurrence in history.

Could it be that Shostakovich felt more in tune with the new regime? Or was he simply exhausted by the years of struggle and prepared to capitulate? Khrushchev had ousted Beria in July 1953 and reunited the MGB (security and intelligence) and MVD (law enforcement) powers to create the Komitet Gosudarstvennoy Bezopasnosti, which, under its all-too-familiar initials, remained the feared arm of Soviet internal and external security until the dramatic break-up of 1991. In February 1956, Khrushchev gave his famous Secret Speech to the Twentieth Congress of the Soviet Communist Party. In it, for the first time, he expressed disquiet about Stalin's 'errors'. Yet any sign that Soviet society might be liberalising was tempered by brutal repressions elsewhere in the Soviet bloc. As the Central Committee signed an agreement to eliminate the 'cult of personality' – Khrushchev's ally Georgy Zhukov would shortly fall victim to this change, being accused of having a 'Bonaparte complex' and forced into retirement – Russian tanks were crushing an uprising in Poland. That same October, the Hungarian uprising was put down with overwhelming force by the Red Army. Some 30,000 died; throughout the West, loyal Popular Front Communists tearfully tore up their party cards, while Communist-sympathising 'fellow travellers' quietly put away their Marxist–Leninist texts. In 1949, *The God That Failed*, a collection of confessional essays edited by the British anti-Communist politician Richard Crossman, documented a generation's disillusionment with Popular Front Communism now that God was revealed to be a destroying juggernaut.

This was not a world in which a composer of Shostakovich's stamp could afford to be complacent. And yet the String Quartet No. 6 in G major seems to inhabit a lighter, blander world than any of its predecessors. Again, it relies in its opening measures on a certain false simplicity that only gradually and subtly begins to reveal its satirical edge. The cheerful bucolic dances, with just a few belching interruptions from what still sounds like the old Stalin figure, are steadily revealed to be contrived, forced. Stalin may be gone, but in his place there comes a subtler propaganda. Instead of repression, self-repression; instead of rigorous Five-Year Plans, photographs of smiling peasants and folk-dance troupes – while, elsewhere, armies still march, dissidents are still taken, the Gulag still functions. Evil recurs.

The idea of recurrence also figured strongly in the Symphony No. 11 in G minor. It is one of Shostakovich's largest scores, with forces that rival the Seventh Symphony, and possibly for that reason has suffered a more lasting neglect in the West, criticised for bombast and shallowness. It is perhaps his most unashamedly populist work, cast in four continuous movements, attacca, with celesta and bells sounding a powerful tocsin in the final movement. As previously mentioned, its subtitle, *The Year 1905*, was dismissed by the British composer Michael Tippett as an 'alibi', and Shostakovich himself made it clear (albeit inconsistently) that his symphony was about contemporary reality every bit as much as it related to that tragic failed people's revolution that had engaged his family's hopes so wholeheartedly fifty years before and just months before his own conception.

A family member disclosed that the original manuscript of the Eleventh Symphony read '1906' and not the year before. This, of course, was the date of Shostakovich's birth, suggesting that he intended the work to be a kind of requiem, not just for himself but for a generation too young to have resisted the corruption of the earlier revolution's democratic promise. The folk songs woven into the score, notably 'Slushai' ('Listen and Take Heed') and 'Arrestant' ('The Prisoner'), were among those that he would have heard at the family piano. The martial sound of the allegro second movement, including one of Shostakovich's most vigorous marches, has a quality that is subtly different to the marches of old, though it hearkens back to the same bygone time and a purer revolutionary spirit. The contrast between that time – as represented by his parents' generation – and the present could hardly have been starker. Much was happening in 1956. Political prisoners were returning from the Gulag, many of them damaged and living only shadowy half-lives. If the regime seemed to have softened in its internal politics, it had simply turned its fury outward, as the suppression of the Polish and Hungarian uprisings attested. Shostakovich himself denied that the symphony was intended to reference events in Budapest, insisting that it was, indeed, about the 1905 revolution, but he was by then a master of the double perspective and perfectly capable of alluding to one event while ostensibly focusing on another. All works, even the most elegiac and nostalgic, are in some way concerned with present-day reality; after all, elegy in the modern sense presupposes a past that is gone, and nostalgia rather depends on a negative comparison between past and present.

Listening to the Eleventh Symphony now, the impression is less of bombast (the perennial complaint of Western critics) than of disappointment, albeit couched in what sounds like exaggerated optimism and passion. Shostakovich seems to have regarded the ultimately partial 1905 revolution and the tragedy of 22 January, Bloody Sunday, when troops fired on hungry protesters, as a 'what if?' moment in which events could just as easily have gone in another direction, had the tsar opened his granaries and food stores. The crowd led by Father Georgy Gapon wanted dialogue, a chance to petition Nicholas

II in a moment of desperate need. Tragically, the Imperial Guard saw only threat and opened fire, killing perhaps 200 souls (the exact figure wavers up and down) and wounding up to 800 more. It was a dark moment for the infant revolution, but also a turning point in Romanov fortunes. From that moment onward, the revolutionary clock was ticking. New political urgencies were already in the saddle, and the great democratic breakthrough, when it came, was either stillborn or deformed, depending on point of view.

Though ostensibly inspired by Mussorgsky's populism, always a benchmark in Shostakovich's music, the Eleventh Symphony exudes even more of Tchaikovsky's doomed romanticism. The number three is everywhere, as always when Shostakovich wants to evoke the people, but here it is 'the people' in abstract form, people who, in the version given in *Testimony*, 'have stopped believing because the cup of evil has run over'. At the very moment the regime was proposing that all echelons of society would benefit from some exposure to everyday labour – except the Politburo, needless to say – the people's composer seemed to have made an icon of them. Not surprisingly, the Eleventh Symphony was a resounding popular success, which is perhaps why it is so little regarded now.

Shostakovich seemed, for the moment, insulated from criticism. His fiftieth birthday on 25 September 1956 was recognised with the Order of Lenin. He was also made an honorary member of the St Cecilia Academy in Italy, one of the world's oldest musical institutions. Immediately after the Twentieth Congress of the Soviet Communist Party, discussions began as to whether the infamous 1948 decree on formalism in music should be rescinded or at least re-evaluated. It was another two years before the Central Committee released an edict with the abbreviated title 'On the Correction of Errors'. Its full title mentioned the work of other, now obscure, composers, but did not directly refer to Shostakovich. Nevertheless, it formally ended Shostakovich's decade of critical ostracism. He was even asked to give a reply and vote of thanks to Khrushchev at a Kremlin reception for writers and intellectuals, a duty that would more naturally have fallen to Khrennikov. That put an official stamp on what was clearly a process of gradual rehabilitation, which had sped up when Shostakovich was asked to chair the jury of the internationally prestigious Tchaikovsky Competition. To have an unperson in such a role would have been unthinkable.

One thing soured his return to favour. The thought that his beloved *Lady Macbeth of Mtsensk* might be revived was worth more to Shostakovich than a whole chest of medals, and probably more than all the other works suppressed under the Zhdanov decree. The shadow of the *Pravda* article still hung over the treasured opera. In the spring of 1955, however, he responded to a request from the Maly Opera in Leningrad and played a somewhat revised version of the opera to its directorate. As a result, Shostakovich was advised to make a direct application to Molotov, then the first deputy chair of the Communist party (but soon to be removed by Khrushchev for belonging to an 'anti-party group'), for *Lady Macbeth of Mtsensk* to be cleared for performance. Shostakovich had returned to the score and made substantial changes. There was a suspiciously long delay – during which Shostakovich was partly distracted by preparations for the long-delayed premiere by Oistrakh and Mravinsky of the Violin Concerto No. 1 in A minor – but an audition of the revised work was arranged for 11 and 12 March 1956. The fact that Central Committee members were prepared to come to Shostakovich's apartment at Mozhayskoye Highway rather than summon him to the Composers' Union augured well. Cultural politics in Russia was always a matter of tiny omens and subliminal hints. Artists learned, like shepherds and sailors, to listen, watch, and even smell the tiniest changes in weather. Life and professional wellbeing could depend on them. For his part, Shostakovich insisted that *Katerina Ismailova* (as the revised version of the opera is known) should be sharply dissociated from the work that had prompted 'Muddle Instead of Music'. Unfortunately, his listeners reiterated the complaints of the infamous editorial almost word for word, condemning the opera's content and the animalistic tone of the score. *Katerina Ismailova* was not cleared for performance for another seven years, and even then was put on in absurdly clandestine circumstances, disguised on posters as *The Barber of Seville*.

When this blow came, expected but still shocking, in 1956, Shostakovich simply straightened himself on the sofa where he had slumped after playing through the opera and thanked his listeners, fellow musicians all, for their 'criticisms'.

Nine

Shostakovich's real response to the absurdities of the Zhdanov decree and its aftermath was probably hidden away in *Rayok*, the satirical cantata he based on Mussorgsky's own 'peep show', lampooning his contemporaries. There is some doubt about the exact dating and circumstances of the work, but Lebedinsky – who claims to have written the libretto – dates it to the Second Congress of the Composers' Union, which took place in the spring of 1957. The apparent stimulus was the inability of a Central Committee official to pronounce the name of the composer Rimsky-Korsakov correctly, this awkwardness dropping from the lips of a man with direct responsibility for cultural matters. That official, Dmitri Shepilov, along with the musicologist Pavel Apostolov, Zakharov, Zhdanov, and Stalin himself, is quoted in the work, as is a Georgian folk song that was supposed to have been a favourite of the late *vozhd*. Appended to the score is a mock-official rider 'to help students' that portrays the work as dramatising the struggle between realism and formalism. Satire often relies on the conceit of the 'found document', and Shostakovich's imaginary publisher (as if such a work could have been published!) claims to have discovered it buried in shit.

Rayok – also known as *Portrait Gallery* – was first performed in January 1989 in Washington DC, with Mstislav Rostropovich conducting. Like many of Shostakovich's friends, Rostropovich did not believe that a work of such open contempt for the regime could have been written any earlier than 1957, and certainly not in 1948 (the other suggested date), when Stalin was still alive and Shostakovich was living under the cloud of criticism and fear generated by the First Congress of the Composers' Union. Rostropovich did not seem to doubt, however, that the work, which is fairly meretricious in purely musical terms, was the work of Shostakovich alone and not an 'exquisite corpse' passed among friends as a dangerously subversive parlour game. Musically, at least, it does not suggest the work of several hands.

There are questions about the exact authorship of *Katerina Ismailova* as well. Isaac Glikman claimed to have had a hand in the revisions to Shostakovich's opera, and some observers have seen in its later, published version the hand of Irina Supinskaya, who worked on the literary side at the Sovietsky Kompozitor publishing house and who, in December 1962, four years after their first meeting, became Shostakovich's third wife. Their marriage came shortly after the premiere of Shostakovich's controversial Thirteenth Symphony, and from then till the end Irina was his loyal supporter and helpmeet.

Almost thirty years Shostakovich's junior (and thus almost his daughter's age), Irina was petite, bespectacled, and attractive rather than beautiful, and she had a curious burr in her speech that led her to muddle *l* and *r* sounds. No one had quite understood the attraction of Margarita Kainova, other than her resemblance to Nina. With Irina, it was much more obvious. She was vibrant, clever, and obviously devoted to 'Mitya', and her history could only have moved his heart. Born in Leningrad, she had seen her father swept up in the Great Terror, while her grandparents died during the siege. Irina had been raised in one of the state orphanages – the Communist party's version of Magdalene houses – reserved for dissident families. In addition, as a seven-year-old, she had been evacuated to Kuibyshev, where the Shostakovich children had spent the war and where the Seventh Symphony was first performed. Her only shortcoming was that she was married when she and Shostakovich first met.

Irina helped prepare the definitive version of *Katerina Ismailova* for publication and also worked on the published text of *Moscow, Cheryomushki*, a comic operetta written in 1958 about the new high-rise flats that Khrushchev was throwing up all over Moscow for workers and minor officials. Ironically, the building in 1961 of a new tower block to house the Composers' Union meant that Shostakovich (soon to be joined by Irina) moved into apartments in the Composers' Union's old building, the very place where he had suffered his deepest personal and professional humiliations.

If he seemed happier and more youthful, the appearance was deceptive. The Shostakovich who revisited the United States, and visited Central America, in 1959 was no more vital and relaxed a man than the pale, nervous figure of the previous decade, but on this occasion he was travelling in company with the hated Khrennikov and was required to give cheerleading answers to questions about Russian music and Russian society. A 2007 Tim Jones poem, 'Shostakovich in

America', published in *Bravado* magazine, imagines the composer cutting loose from his minders (cleverly disguised as Kappa Gamma Beta frat boys) on this trip and exploring the hinterland in a chauffeur-driven DeSoto, even curling up 'in a co-ed's bed', but all the same never far from 'the Kremlin', 'the bottle of Georgian wine', and 'the black telephone'.

Whether Shostakovich was happy in America or not, he spent that summer working on the Cello Concerto No. 1 in E-flat major, which was premiered in Leningrad on 4 October, with its dedicatee Rostropovich as soloist and Mravinsky as conductor. In contrast to the work of previous years, it is alert and open writing, with a vividness of touch and a new confidence even in its satirical elements, as when the same Georgian folk song used to make fun of Stalin in *Rayok* is quoted again.

The concerto is also a work of notable structural simplicity, based on a single theme that grows organically through both the solo and orchestral parts. Again, the D–S–C–H motif is evident. In Rostropovich, the composer had found the perfect conduit for his work, an 'instrumental' voice of genuinely democratic power. Because he could rely on Rostropovich's formidable technique, he was emboldened to include some difficult solo material and rhythmic subtleties, in part inspired by Prokofiev's relatively recent Symphony-Concerto in E minor, also for cello and orchestra. As well as Shostakovich's motif, there are references to folk music (a Mussorgsky lullaby in the first movement) and, in the final section, a sardonic reference to one of Stalin's favourite songs (which had also figured in *Rayok*).

There was a further dimension to the relationship of composer and cellist at this time. Shostakovich and Rostropovich had performed regularly on tour in the Soviet Union, and in 1957 they decided to record one of the staples of their repertoire, Shostakovich's joyous Cello Sonata in D minor from 1934, for the state recording label, Melodiya. Unexpectedly, Shostakovich had difficulty executing some of the right-hand chords, and Rostropovich had to help him out. Shostakovich mentions his friend very little in *Testimony*, and not until towards the end. But he does state that Rostropovich can do 'anything', by which he doesn't just mean everything in music. In Shostakovich's eyes, his friend's omnicompetence is a deeply Russian trait and the key to his ability to rise to any and every challenge. Shostakovich had begun to suffer pain in his hand the previous year and, after the problem continued to worsen, he was hospitalised for treatment in January 1960. His career as a performer was in jeopardy. For years, he had been the main interpreter of his own Piano Concerto No. 1, written during the rehearsals for *Lady Macbeth of Mtsensk*. It was the first significant piano concerto of the Soviet era and was written at a time when Shostakovich could still risk a confrontational attitude in his music. He gave the premiere with the Leningrad Philharmonic in October 1933 and continued to play the music – which had originally been intended as a trumpet concerto; it survives in the mournful reprise of the slow movement – until physical constraints forced him to stop.

Shostakovich wrote a substantial amount of music in 1960, including one of his unquestioned masterpieces, and that crabbed, painful hand also inscribed a signature on one of the most controversial documents of Shostakovich's career: an application to join the Communist party. As a purely personal decision it seems mystifying, and it was a shock to his friends. Membership of the Communist party was not comparable to, say, membership of the Nazi party in Germany during the war years, when non-membership was a sign of dissent. On the contrary, a Communist party card was a privilege that had to be earned. One showed one's worthiness through conformity to Soviet ideals; that these were subject to sea-change merely laid down further challenges to the loyalist. After years of stoical resistance, was Shostakovich capitulating? Some even claimed that he had been drunk when he signed a pre-filled form, and thus had no real hand in the 'application'. Given his record, before and since, of signing documents he had not read or could not possibly approve, this is not outside the realms of possibility. He had rather cravenly put his name to an official condemnation of novelist Aleksandr Solzhenitsyn and physicist Andrei Sakharov, one of the pioneers of the Soviet H-bomb. In context, the decision to apply is somewhat less strange. Khrushchev wanted to attract leading intellectuals to the party, largely to counter an impression in the West that all Russian artists were automatically 'dissident'. There were limits to the new leader's tolerance, and they certainly did not stretch to Pasternak, who had been awarded the Nobel Prize in Literature in 1958 but had been forced to renounce *Doctor Zhivago* (and the laureateship) shortly before being expelled from the Writers' Union. For the last two years of his life – Pasternak died at the end of May 1960 – he was hounded mercilessly by the authorities.

There was much in common, as well as many differences, between the two artists. Perhaps most important of all was their shared commitment to their respective crafts. Pasternak continued to write, even under the greatest pressure. Likewise Shostakovich, who could not delegate a single aspect of the creative process, worked on doggedly in ill health. Shostakovich, however, was increasingly seen as an establishment figure. He was invited to give composition masterclasses to postgraduate students at the Leningrad Conservatory and would later be elected to the Supreme Soviet of the USSR – but, in the meantime, the condition of his election as chair of the Composers' Union was that he joined the party. He was accepted as a candidate member in September 1960 – the immediate reward was that the Eighth Symphony was allowed back into the repertory – and received his full party card the following autumn. But even this descended into farce. So nervous was Shostakovich of the step he was taking that he left Moscow for Leningrad shortly before the admission was to take place and took refuge with his sister, sending a sick note to apologise for his absence. He seems to have gone through a suicidal episode after making his application. Lebedinsky, an old Bolshevik who had long since lost faith in the Soviet system, remembers confiscating sleeping pills from him.

These feelings suggest a context for the great works of 1960. Coming in order of completion between the Seventh and Eighth Quartets was a work for voice and piano, the openly dissident *Satires*. This work Shostakovich cautiously subtitled *Pictures of the Past*. The Moscow audience demanded two full-length encores when the composer and soprano Galina

Vishnevskaya gave the premiere in February 1961. The texts were taken from the work of the poet and children's writer Sasha Chorny, the pen-name of Alexander Glikberg, who had left Russia after the revolution and who died in France in 1932, while fighting a fire. The wartime firefighter Shostakovich had read Chorny's poems while evacuated to Kuibyshev, but the stimulus to write something around them had to wait until anti-Semitism was no longer a plank of state policy – Chorny was a Jew – but also until he had found a voice as flexible and beautiful as Vishnevskaya's. Formerly a music-hall singer, the Bolshoi's leading soprano had made her name as Tosca and Violetta – doubtless Shostakovich had heard her as Katerina Ismailova in his dreams; she later played the role in Mikhail Shapiro's 1966 film version – and was married to Rostropovich. The couple fell foul of the Soviet authorities when they harboured Solzhenitsyn in their summer house; they left the Soviet Union the year before Shostakovich's death and were stripped of citizenship four years later.

Shostakovich wrote other pieces for Vishnevskaya. The soprano part in the Fourteenth Symphony was inspired by her, and she was the composer's chosen interpreter for his orchestration of Mussorgsky's *Songs and Dances of Death* (also heard at the sensational February 1961 concert and orchestrated the following year) and the *Seven Romances on Poems by Alexander Blok* five years after that. However, *Satires* should not be underestimated relative to these more prominent works. The piece and the reaction to it show that Shostakovich was still understood – and, more importantly, understood himself – to be playing a double game, conforming in outward particulars while still cocking a snook at Soviet society behind the guise of a costume drama.

In contrast to *Satires*, the first of the 1960 string quartets is so personal a work that it scarcely seems fit for public performance at all, and were it not such a masterpiece of structural control it might well be allowed to sit apart from the official sequence of Shostakovich's chamber works. The String Quartet No. 7 in F-sharp minor is very short, just under twelve minutes in length, and consists of three connected movements. Its changes of mood – brisk, buoyant opening; slightly desolate middle section; and dramatic, anxiety-ridden third movement before the opening subject returns in apotheosis – are easy enough to decode when one reads the work's superscription to the late Nina Vasilyevna. This is Shostakovich's musical farewell to his late wife. Even Ingmar Bergman could not deliver such a condensed portrait of a marriage and its strains. The opening is a wholly convincing sound-picture of the bright, combative woman remembered by friends. The movement's developing tensions are consistent with the volatile nature of the marriage. The middle movement hints at separation, interrupted abruptly by Nina's decline and Shostakovich's hectic flight to Armenia to see her before she died. The return of the opening theme sees her spirit triumphant over death. There are other possible readings, and of course it is possible to read the work entirely as a triumphant exercise in form, but it would be perverse to ignore the autobiographical element and the emotion that attended it.

Its successor is also unmistakably autobiographical, and in some respects represents a companion piece. Shostakovich seemed to regard the Eighth Quartet as a memorial to himself, undertaken in a spirit somewhere between self-pity and defiance. He characterised its mood to Glikman as 'pseudo-tragedy' – self-deprecation? the *yurodivy* speaking again? – and described how, while composing it, his 'tears flowed as abundantly as urine after downing half a dozen beers'. This might sound like bathos, but the Russian spirit refuses to entertain a distinction between higher and lower feelings. Simple bodily functions and high emotion are often treated in exactly the same way. The tears came again when he played it through after returning home, though this time they were prompted not by the 'pseudo-tragedy' but in admiration of his own wonderful unity of form. One often encounters Shostakovich as first audience of his own work, unaware of its impact until it is finished and realised in performance.

Apart from the Fifth and Seventh Symphonies, none of Shostakovich's works has been subject to such scrutiny as the String Quartet No. 8 in C minor. The work was largely written in East Germany, where in July 1960 Shostakovich visited Dresden. The city had been the target of the notorious Allied firebombing of February 1945 in which 25,000 were killed. His ostensible purpose was to write soundtrack music for a film, *Five Days, Five Nights*. For all the apparently vulgar diffidence of his comments, Shostakovich was clearly moved by the suffering of the people and by the destruction, in the burning of the city itself, of one of the symbols of Baroque humanism. The Eighth Quartet bears the inscription 'In memory of the victims of fascism' and is often referred to as the Dresden Quartet, particularly in Russia. As ever, the inscription is double-edged; one might argue that the people of Dresden were victims of the free West, or that 'fascism' applies equally to Soviet totalitarianism.

If Shostakovich was a dissembler, this is him in excellent form, because what one hears in the work when primed with that purely circumstantial title is a sound-picture of war, complete with droning glissandi to represent the sirens and great bursts of sound to suggest the brutal ordinance that set off Dresden's firestorm. It suited the Khrushchev regime very well that a rehabilitated formalist should have contributed a work that so clearly expressed solidarity with the wartime suffering of an enemy and that was so bracingly 'realist' in approach. But is that really what the Eighth Quartet is about? The film music written in Dresden carries very little sign of strong emotion. Take away the programmatic title and superscription, and the Eighth Quartet turns into one of Shostakovich's most personal and self-referential works, a curiously wrought autobiographical monument. Writing to Glikman, Shostakovich suggested that the real title should be 'Dedicated to the author of this quartet', and listed all the self-references contained in this 'little miscellany', another intriguingly diffident description for one of his own most important works.

The quartet begins with the now familiar D–S–C–H monogram but very soon quotes the First, Fifth, Eighth, and Tenth Symphonies; the piano trio; the cello concerto; and *Lady Macbeth of Mtsensk*, all works with a profound resonance for their creator. In addition, it alludes to Wagner (several of whose works were first performed in Dresden), specifically the funeral march from *Götterdämmerung*, and the first movement of Tchaikovsky's *Pathétique Symphony*. What, Shostakovich rhetorically asks in *Testimony*, do any of these have to do with fascism? With the possible exception of the Wagner, one has to say: nothing. Unless, that is, one accepts the possibility (noted by Lebedinsky) that Shostakovich considered himself one of the victims of state fascism, and that the references back to the prison songs of *Lady Macbeth of Mtsensk* and to the old revolutionary song 'Tormented by Grievous Bondage' were a way of signifying that Shostakovich himself had lived in a state of virtual captivity. In that case, the Eighth Quartet's public and private meanings precisely intersect.

When the new party member decided to give the subtitle *The Year 1917* to his Twelfth Symphony, written in the summer of 1961, it looked as though his capitulation and assimilation were complete. The 'Lenin symphony' he had used as a smokescreen in 1938 seemed to have become an embarrassing reality, though it has been suggested that the original intention was to write a work that caricatured and satirised Lenin – an unthinkable heresy. Shostakovich could not overcome a visceral conviction that Stalinism was merely Leninism with a Georgian accent. He had always made it clear that Lenin, too, was a tyrant and that he despised the hagiographers who had turned him into an otherworldly spirit. That is alluded to in the strangely hymn-like melody that seems to identify Lenin in the Twelfth Symphony, but which constantly slips back into a more earthly register when confronted with the kind of material that always signals 'the people' in Shostakovich's work. And there is a reference to a very early work, something Shostakovich did ever more frequently in his last years, most notably in the viola sonata, his last catalogued work, where he takes in the whole sweep of his career with a single reference. Here, it is more pointed, an allusion to the *Funeral March for the Victims of the Revolution*, where all of Shostakovich's ambivalence – hope soured by violence, liberty trampled by authority – is brought into play.

The Twelfth Symphony is a curious work, not so much employing irony as utterly wrapped in it. Shostakovich conceded that the material offered up 'resistance' and that the work was not a success, beginning with one creative goal and ending up somewhere else entirely; his explanation of what that original goal might have been isn't entirely clear. Somewhat like the Eighth Quartet, this symphony needs to be understood in a quite specific context. When it was given its first British performance, at the Edinburgh Festival in 1962, listeners were appalled by its sardonic tone. The present writer's father heard it on that occasion and was dismayed. The irony had been inaudible at the première because the work had been chosen to be played at the Twenty-second Congress of the Soviet Communist Party, just a few weeks before Shostakovich was accorded full party membership. This was the setting for Khrushchev's second attack on Stalin, which led to the *vozhd's* remains being removed from their place of pilgrimage in Red Square. In future, only Lenin was to be the object of such veneration. Shostakovich, who had suffered under Stalin, had grasped the zeitgeist by seeming to deliver at last on the promise of a 'Lenin symphony' (even if it was no such thing). Once again, self-serving logic had come up with an acceptable equation of politics and creativity. Once again, fresh disproof was just around the corner.

Ten

Twelve weeks after the premiere of the Twelfth Symphony – to a spectrum of reactions that would eventually run from official approval to public indifference at home and outright hostility abroad – an earlier, more cherished work was eventually brought out into the light. On the penultimate day of 1961, Kirill Kondrashin – whom Shostakovich had come to trust as much as Mravinsky – gave the downbeat that began the belated first performance of Shostakovich's Symphony No. 4 in C minor, which had been written, rehearsed, and abandoned half a lifetime earlier. Along with *Lady Macbeth of Mtsensk*, it is one of the composer's masterpieces. It may be that the work's revival was a sop to Shostakovich in return for the relatively conformist Twelfth Symphony. There was perhaps a growing coolness between Shostakovich and Mravinsky, who had always been his conductor of choice, but who had a lofty manner and a mandarin disregard for others. Rostropovich found him arrogant and remote. Without naming him, Shostakovich says in *Testimony* that 'the man who considers himself its greatest interpreter does not understand my music'. Mravinsky's insistence that Shostakovich 'could not' write affirmative finales to the Fifth and Seventh Symphonies annoyed him: 'It never occurred to this man that

I never thought about any exultant finales, because what exultation could there be?' It seems that, under the influence of his wife, Mravinsky had declined to conduct the Thirteenth Symphony, fearing its content. In Kondrashin, Shostakovich had found not just a substitute but a conductor passionately committed to the music as the composer wrote it.

For the moment, though, the problem with the Fourth Symphony was finding the music. The score had been lost during the war, possibly burnt to heat the Leningrad apartment during the siege. Some orchestral parts were discovered in the city, though, and Shostakovich undertook to examine them and to create a piano reduction. It was assumed, not least by Shostakovich himself, that he would have to make substantial revisions, but he told Kondrashin that he was happy with the work as it stood, and the Fourth Symphony was put into rehearsal, without this time the problem of a frightened and obstructive conductor.

The reaction of one listener is telling. Shostakovich had met the scientist Flora Litvinova and her husband Mikhail Litvinov while evacuated to Kuibyshev. She was one of the old friends that Shostakovich invited to the premiere. Litvinova was stunned and somewhat discomfited: 'Why do Dmitri Dmitriyevich's later works lack those qualities of impetuosity, dynamic drive, contrasts of rhythm and colour, tenderness, and spikiness?' It was not an entirely rhetorical question, for Litvinova goes on to blame 'the "historic" Decree which warped the living spirit in him'.

Warped, but did not break. The revival of the Fourth Symphony and the evergreen hope of seeing *Katerina Ismailova* staged again seemed to light new fires in Shostakovich. His creative energies and reputation had both oscillated wildly since the Great Terror years, but rarely in synchronisation. Now that he had won official approval with a relatively weak symphonic work, it seemed inevitable that he would again face criticism for a great one.

The Soviet literary scene had changed even more dramatically than music during the thaw years. In 1962, on the advice of Aleksandr Tvardovsky (who had been restored to his position as editor of the literary magazine *Novy Mir* during the second thaw), Khrushchev personally authorised the publication in *Novy Mir* of Solzhenitsyn's *One Day in the Life of Ivan Denisovich*, which became an international success in translation. Solzhenitsyn, though, was nearly fifty and had clear memories of the Great Terror, which coloured his later actions and statements, and which, during his American exile, amounted to 'a plague on both your houses'. By the turn of the 1960s, a new generation of writers had come forward with no such memories and with relatively high expectations of creative freedom, and they would feel any backlash all the more keenly as a consequence.

One of them was the poet Yevgeny Yevtushenko, still not thirty years of age in 1962 but already widely admired and clearly the rising star of the new literary generation. Born in Siberia to a once-noble family of complex descent, with Polish, German, and Tatar forebears, he adopted his mother's name rather than the original family name of Gangnus. After extensive travel in Siberia with his geologist parents, Yevtushenko came to post-war Moscow and began establishing a reputation as a poet whose work boldly confronted controversial social and historical issues. In September 1961, his long poem 'Babi Yar', which told of the Nazi massacre of many thousands of Ukrainian Jews at a ravine outside the city of Kiev in September 1941, was published in *Literaturnaya Gazeta*. The poem's importance lay in Yevtushenko's insistence that the massacre wasn't simply another wartime atrocity but a specific act of genocide directed against Ukraine's Jews. Shostakovich read it shortly after the premiere of the Twelfth Symphony, still smarting from his work's weirdly reversed reception – official approval, disappointment among friends and supporters. Yevtushenko had already emerged as the bellwether of intelligent youthful dissidence, so Shostakovich telephoned him to suggest that he might make a setting of 'Babi Yar'. It was a huge vote of confidence for a young writer, and Yevtushenko enthusiastically accepted, providing Shostakovich with other texts and, ultimately, with a specially written poem. Even so, as Shostakovich revealed later, the young poet had some doubts about the older composer's moral fibre, asking him awkward questions, presumably about his willingness to accede to political demands. Shostakovich, in his studiously diffident way, affected not to like Yevtushenko's later work quite so much.

The usual narrative is that Shostakovich initially intended to write a cantata based on 'Babi Yar', but there is evidence that he saw in the poem some potential both to neutralise the disappointment of his Twelfth Symphony and to moderate his old suspicion of Proletkult song-symphonies and verbal apotheoses by including a vocal part for only the second time in his symphonic career. One misleading conception of 'Babi Yar' is that it only concerns the massacre. That is untrue beyond the first movement. In subsequent movements – 'Humour', 'In the Shop', 'Fears', and 'A Career' – Shostakovich and Yevtushenko deal with wider issues, not least the atmosphere that pervaded Russia during the pre-war Great Terror. It seemed impossible that such a work could avoid controversy, even in a somewhat relaxed new political climate.

Nothing complicated the censorship situation in Russia more than the immediate success of Solzhenitsyn's short novel. Widely admired and recognised as an officially sanctioned memoir of the bad old days, it let loose a flood of bottom-drawer manuscripts, journals, and thinly disguised autobiographical fictions that immediately put Khrushchev's tentative moratorium on censorship into reverse. A slow trickle of thaw was one thing, a torrent something else. In December 1962, the leader visited an exhibition called Thirty Years of Moscow Art and launched an astonishing attack on contemporary culture, calling many of the artists represented in the show 'pederasts', by which it is assumed he meant 'masturbators'. An even more thoroughgoing vulgarian than Stalin, and surrounded by philistine advisers, Khrushchev did not seem to understand what was meant by 'abstraction' in art, using the word as an insult for anything he disliked. Shortly afterwards, despite the cachet of having his poem 'The Heirs of Stalin' published in *Pravda*, Yevtushenko was attacked by one of Khrushchev's henchmen at a Kremlin reception for writers. Leonid Ilyichyov, the former *Izvestia* newspaper editor and recent head of agitprop and propaganda at the

Central Committee, objected to the implication in 'Babi Yar' that only Jews, and not countless thousands of Slavs, had died in the Nazi Holocaust. Soviet anti-Semitism reared up again. Though later he submitted to pressure and reworked the poem, bringing down on his head the wrath of liberal intellectuals, Yevtushenko on this occasion bravely stood up to Khrushchev himself, even after the leader had growled an old country proverb about the grave curing cripples, a plain reference to the feeling that the best way of dealing with those warped by dissidence was simply to liquidate them. More alarmingly for Shostakovich, Ilyichyov expressed disgust that such nonsense as 'Babi Yar' had been set to music. The regime had cleared the way to suppress the Thirteenth Symphony, then in rehearsal under Kondrashin.

Shostakovich had begun work on the score in June, after a short period in hospital. He finished the symphony in August, shortly before leaving for the Edinburgh Festival. It was clear on his return that there would be problems with the work, but rehearsals proceeded, even after the first choice for bass soloist was ruled out and his replacement was conveniently called away to sing a role for the Bolshoi. It seems others may have been approached, but the word was out that the role was a poisoned chalice; one after another, singers dropped out with contrived excuses, apparently nervous about the material and how it might affect their own performing career. Shostakovich said they behaved 'shamefully, shamefully'. But, perhaps stiffened by the renewed international fame and notional protection from harm that the visit to Edinburgh had brought Shostakovich, he and his circle seemed bent on confrontation.

Once again, as he had with the first violin concerto and other works of 1948, Shostakovich chose to identify strongly with the Jews. One of the passages later revised by Yevtushenko begins, 'I feel I am a Jew', and expresses an imaginative empathy with Christ on the cross – an astonishing projection for Shostakovich, a lifelong atheist, to make. Once again, in seeming to write about other subjects and other times, he created an excoriating portrait of his own country in the present tense. Though inevitably much of the emphasis surrounding the Thirteenth Symphony was and remains directed to its text, the musical language and codes are immediately familiar, drawing somewhat on Mussorgsky's opera *Khovanshchina*. Power is represented by thudding two-note fortes, the people by threes. There is ample quotation from earlier work, significantly from the Sixth Quartet, and yet the unities of the score seem forced in comparison with the recently revived Fourth Symphony. Given the disparity of its musical sources, the main sense of unity comes from Yevtushenko rather than Shostakovich.

On 18 December 1962, the symphony was greeted with wild acclaim in Moscow, though the official boxes remained conspicuously empty, as party officials stayed away to write their reports without the awkward prejudice of having actually listened to the piece. To a sophisticated metropolitan audience, it was as if Shostakovich had put aside his temporising and his enwrapped ambiguities and written this time passionately from the heart. The association with a hot-blooded young writer raised the composer's credit, but also served to disguise the sombre nature of the scoring. Shostakovich's unadorned later style and aura of blank fatalism – 'tragedy' is no longer the right word – can be traced to the fustian scoring of 'In the Shop', where he portrays a world of shortages, queues, tasteless greyness.

For the moment, though, this was not of outward concern to the composer, who seemed to ride out the ensuing storm with Yevtushenko as his human shield. He had, in any case, other things to look forward to: marriage to Irina and, in late December and January, the long-awaited revival of *Lady Macbeth of Mtsensk/Katerina Ismailova*.

Though Shostakovich's music is all very much of a piece and difficult to divide up stylistically, the Thirteenth Symphony ushered in what was unmistakably a 'late period', marked by slow, spacious music, punctuated by silences, but also with sharp percussion (which was probably the result of reworking the clangorous Fourth Symphony) and characterised by what in any other composer might be described as spirituality, if not religiosity. The tolling of church bells in the Thirteenth Symphony strikes an unexpected note. Flora Litvinova's comment about the preceding symphony is perhaps best treated as description rather than criticism. Much of the nervous vitality – the hectic village dances and the songs that cocked a snook at authority in all its forms – had disappeared. Some attribute this sense of enervation to ill health and particularly to the problems with his right hand. Others have assumed that it was an understandable reaction to the rigours and anxieties of the preceding thirty years, a chastening experience even for a more rugged individual. And yet, when one looks at Shostakovich's life in the round, it is his strength and stoicism that stand out, not any sign of constitutional weakness.

Listening to the works of the final period, one hears a steadily deepening absorption in sound itself. The music becomes less linear, more meditative, and at times almost sculptural in its stillness. Shostakovich never approaches the massive sustains and repetitions of his pupil Ustvolskaya, whose intensely spiritual, almost static 'symphonies' for small instrumental groups were also subject to de facto proscription and only became widely known in the 1980s. A whole generation of composers influenced by Shostakovich was emerging. Born in 1934, Alfred Schnittke had taken up the challenge of Shostakovich's implicit polystylistics and was embarked on a body of work that would recapture something of the master's sardonic energy. His earliest works, the violin concerto of 1957 and the oratorio *Nagasaki*, show little sign of a direct debt, though in the later concerti grossi – which are postmodernist works written in a deliberately archaic form – Shostakovich's fingerprint can readily be discerned. Schnittke, from Volga German stock, made his name in the West and never had to work under the ideological constraints that had come close to swamping Shostakovich. Rodion Shchedrin, who succeeded him at the Composers' Union, defined himself as 'post-avant-garde' and spent the early part of his career shrewdly brokering a safe establishment position through works like the 1951 piano piece *Festivity on a Collective Farm* and the much later *Solemn Overture* for the sixtieth anniversary of the USSR. Shchedrin grew adept at using his various official positions to camouflage an experimental cosmopolitanism that is perhaps insufficiently appreciated outside Russia.

Shostakovich had learned to perform the same creative sleight-of-hand with far greater subtlety. In the spring of 1964, having met the revered author Mikhail Sholokhov, he announced that he would be writing an opera based on Sholokhov's novel *And Quiet Flows the Don*. Once again, as the choice of subject suggests – he would have thought back wryly to Dzerzhinsky's opera of thirty years before – this was an elaborate charade to distract attention from the work that really occupied him, the forcefully dissonant Ninth and Tenth Quartets.

These were both completed in 1964, a turbulent year for Shostakovich and for Russia. After the severe food shortages of the previous winter, it seemed unlikely that Khrushchev would hang on to power. His deposition in October in favour of the hardliner Leonid Brezhnev would have far-reaching implications for artists and intellectuals, who had grown used to a small degree of liberalisation of expression. For the moment, Brezhnev and his second in command, Alexei Kosygin, were happy to promote the illusion that a further thaw had begun. The metaphor was a doubly meaningful one given the recent harsh winters (which had even brought part of western Europe to a standstill). Shostakovich was, for the moment, able to maintain a carefully adjusted distance from the regime. There was no interruption in the flow of work. He spent much of December and January in the Composers' Union resort at Repino, writing film music for Kozintsev's film of *Hamlet*. This work, Shostakovich's Op. 116, betrays no discernible sign of borrowing from previous *Hamlet* productions. The music is absolutely integral to the film but also stands alone strongly, full of the intense – 'virulent' was the word Kozintsev preferred – philosophical quiddity that marked both subject and composer.

In February, the second Gorky Festival was devoted entirely to Shostakovich's music – a unique retrospective at a time when music festivals were rare and almost unknown in Russia. The accolade was no mere pleasantry but recognition that Shostakovich was now not only the Soviet Union's greatest living composer – the return of Stravinsky for a visit in 1962 did not change that – but also relatively 'safe'.

Shostakovich remained deeply ambivalent towards his exiled countryman, whom he had joined in condemning in 1949. He kept Stravinsky's photograph on his desk and loved his music, while apparently loathing his carelessly worn cosmopolitanism. Stravinsky had actively sought a meeting as soon as he was back on Russian soil; Shostakovich initially avoided any such encounter. When he could no longer avoid the inevitable and had agreed to meet the visitor, he was as nervous and unprepossessing as ever. Some of his unease undoubtedly stemmed from the memory of having colluded, however unwillingly, in Soviet condemnation of Stravinsky. In *Testimony*, he makes his admiration clear – '[Stravinsky is] one of the greatest composers of our times and I truly love many of his works' – though the qualifying words are just as significant. Is 'truly' an attempt to make amends? And does 'many of his works' imply – it surely does – that there was much in Stravinsky's recent output, and particularly the twelve-tone works, that he did not admire at all? There is another explanation for Shostakovich's unease. He never could take a compliment with ease, and nothing would reduce him to a chain-smoking, nail-chewing wreck more than any hint of flattery. After years abroad, Stravinsky now combined Russian passion with an American ease of manner and tendency to boosterism. The informality Shostakovich had disliked on his first visit to America pleased him no more now, especially when it came from a one-time compatriot. The two composers stand to this day in awkward relation – sophisticated and rough-hewn, insouciant and conflicted, but each drawing profoundly in their different ways on both Russian tradition and an international language in music.

If 1964 was to be Shostakovich's last year of virtually full health, he used it productively and with a final flurry of his old obsessions. A cantata, or 'symphonic poem', *The Execution of Stepan Razin*, based on Yevtushenko's poem 'The Bratsk Hydroelectric Station', has all the familiar coding of two against three, authority against people. These same figures appeared again that year, with a later version of the 'betrayal' motif from *Lady Macbeth of Mtsensk*, in the String Quartet No. 9 in E-flat major. This seems to be a transitional work, difficult to distinguish in its faster and more biting passages from any one of a number of previous quartets, but there is also a new quality in the music that suggests history has been transcended. The 'Must it be?'/'It must be!' questions and answers that became part of the language of string quartet writing with Beethoven's late masterpieces no longer refer to earthly or quotidian issues but to the large questions of being and non-being, fate and mortality. Shostakovich burned the first draft in his stove – which, though the gesture shouldn't be overdramatised, tends to counter any suggestion that the work was merely routine and academic, something that could be left in the notebooks to be mined for material later. Clearly, it meant something profound to Shostakovich.

The String Quartet No. 10 in A-flat major compresses much of Shostakovich's composing career into its modest span. More conventional in structure than the Ninth Quartet, it follows the familiar pattern of a quietly untroubled opening cut across by a mordant scherzo, followed by a mourning passacaglia, followed by ambiguous resolution. The only difference is that the final three notes sound very much like someone signing off. The two quartets were premiered together in November 1964. A few weeks later, in the dying days of the year, *The Execution of Stepan Razin* was performed in Moscow. The story is a variation on one that had haunted Shostakovich since he had witnessed the young boy cut down in the street by an uncaring juggernaut authority. Yevtushenko's poem has a thief running through Moscow's streets carrying a poppy-seed roll he has stolen. It is the day of Razin's execution in punishment for leading a Cossack revolt against the powers. As the scene unfolds, the tsar stands squeezing pimples in front of a mirror, admiring a new emerald ring on his hand unsullied by labour. Razin is executed in due course, the sequence of events narrated with pungent brevity, but the beheaded Cossack continues to berate the tsar afterwards, his severed head still spitting defiance. Though its ostensible target was safely circumscribed within revolutionary history, it wasn't difficult to imagine that Yevtushenko and Shostakovich were concerned with more recent and immediate targets of satire than a dynasty that had come to an effective end in the 'House of Special Purpose' forty-six years earlier.

The new year would mark the start of Shostakovich's final decade. He would write two more symphonies, a second violin concerto, five more string quartets (he had hoped to write twenty-four, never repeating a key), and two instrumental masterpieces, one of which would only echo from beyond the grave. Relative longevity was by now his greatest protection. Liquidating young firebrands, as the Razin story underlined, was one thing; disposing of internationally famous composers was a step too far, even for the KGB. The journalist James Cameron once wrote that to describe someone as a survivor was not a compliment, because it implied a life lived defensively rather than boldly and without care of self. Shostakovich's survival to the age of sixty has sometimes been held against him, not least given that so many great talents were swept away by the tides of history, but it is also one of his greatest achievements. Merely to live and to continue to work were themselves small triumphs, not to be underestimated.

Eleven

Shostakovich wrote his final work, the viola sonata, in the summer of 1975, while convalescing from his latest onslaught of illness. He worked, as usual, at Repino. Shostakovich had always hated being asked what his 'last' work was when questioners meant his 'latest', but the viola sonata was a clear-headed and philosophically robust farewell to composition, with an unambiguous nod to Beethoven in the magnificent slow finale. The composer's instructions to the work's dedica-tee and first performer, Fyodor Druzhinin, was that it should sound not morbid or elegiac, but 'bright, bright and clear'.

Shostakovich's last decade was lived in the deepening shadow of ill health. He had never been robust. The privations of the Civil War years had led to tuberculosis and, throughout his life, Shostakovich suffered from psychosomatic illnesses as he converted stress and anxiety into physical symptoms. As he approached his sixtieth birthday, however, his constitution seemed to be breaking down irretrievably. The problem with his hand was eventually diagnosed as poliomyelitis, and Shos-takovich joked wryly about the ailment still being commonly described as 'infantile paralysis'. The affliction had caused him to fall down on several occasions, notably at Maxim's wedding, where he had broken his left leg. A few years later, he broke the other in a car accident while on holiday in Byelorussia, and he limped visibly for the remainder of his days.

A heavy smoker and drinker, he began to suffer heart problems as well, and he was treated in a sanatorium in early 1965 for ischaemia and cardiac occlusion, as well as neurological problems associated with his polio. The following year, he spent some time convalescing at a sanatorium in the Crimea where, forty-two years earlier, he had met his first fiancée, Tanya Glivenko. Worse was to follow. Four months short of his sixtieth birthday, he suffered a severe heart attack and spent the next six weeks at an institution outside Leningrad, in the very same rooms – another grim physical coincidence in his life – where one Andrei Zhdanov had once undergone drying-out treatment.

He was hospitalised again during 1969 and 1970, receiving neurological and cardiological treatment. In September 1971, during rehearsals for his last symphony, there was another significant heart attack. A year later, renal colic and lung cancer were diagnosed, and Shostakovich underwent an intensive course of cobalt radiotherapy that failed to arrest the tumours. News of his illness was kept within the family.

Pain and debility did not seem to change Shostakovich's personality. Always nervous, his face a life's map of tics and twitches, he remained as physically restless and ill-at-ease in unfamiliar company as he had been as a young man. Family friends report that he remained obsessive about tidiness and timekeeping, keeping clocks in his apartment carefully synchronised, tidying his workspace, attending to every detail of his music. His opinions could be harsh and intolerant, and he often affected to forget personal details about people he had known for many years. With relative strangers, he could be laconic and remote and seem almost pathologically shy. Close friends, though, found him warm and dryly funny, with a unstaunchable energy that, when engaged, seemed to lift the years away. They recall the endless games of patience – latterly preferred to the excitement of poker – and Shostakovich's touching habit of noting down football scores in his newspapers as they were announced on the radio.

Shostakovich also proved himself capable of making new friendships, even when the language barrier thwarted intimacy. In 1959 he met Benjamin Britten in London, when they were seated together at the Royal Festival Hall to hear Rostropovich play the first cello concerto. Music was their common language; though temperamentally Britten was very different, his music had much in common with Shostakovich's work in its outward rejection of modernity, or at least its more ideological elements. Three years later, Rostropovich played Britten's cello symphony in Moscow. Over the next few years, Britten and his partner, the tenor Peter Pears, saw a good deal of Shostakovich, spending a happy new year at Zhukova at the beginning of 1967 and on subsequent occasions. In turn, Shostakovich spent part of the summer of 1972 at Britten's home in Aldeburgh, where he began writing his Fourteenth Quartet. In 1973, after receiving radiation therapy, he was well enough to travel once again to the United States and to Britain. His musical horizons also remained wide. He had made unexpected use of serialist elements (still then a virtual orthodoxy in the West) in the Twelfth Quartet, though they remain entirely consistent with its D-flat tonality, but, having stayed faithful to his own vision for more than forty years, he was not ready to do what Stravinsky had done in his late, serialist period and surrender to cosmopolitanism. Shostakovich drew his water from the same well throughout his life.

Though Shostakovich was stoical about most of his physical problems, some were not easy to work around. There was some relief from the problems in his right hand, but as they improved Shostakovich began to feel that his musical imagination was drying up. Though frequently obliged to accept that silence was the safer option, Shostakovich had never before suffered creative block. It is not an affliction invariably associated with age. Unlike in other fields of intellectual activity – mathematics, most notably – a composer's powers tend not to diminish with age, and twentieth-century music is full of opsimaths – among them Elliott Carter and Michael Tippett – who seemed to work with ever greater fluency as they aged, even if they had to contend with unavoidable physical impairments. One such problem troubled Shostakovich deeply. Always myopic, he now began to lose his sight, making work on large scores increasingly difficult. Infirmity revived his interest in Shakespeare's *King Lear.* Thirty years on from his first approach to the play, his Op. 137 of 1970 was used as soundtrack music for Kozintsev's film version; it was the director's last film completing a notional late trilogy that had begun with *Don Quixote* and continued with *Hamlet.* Shostakovich may have felt in a similar position to the aged English king. Perhaps it was time to hand over his position at the head of Russian music to younger and fitter composers, though he was aware – as Lear was not – that the aesthetic values he had lived by might not be upheld by a younger generation. In April 1968, he stood down as first secretary of the Composers' Union. The political and cultural stagnation that had set in during Brezhnev's regime – and would only be swept away by the winds of glasnost and perestroika more than a decade after Shostakovich's death – caused many even among the younger generation to wonder if the game was any longer worth the candle. The Stalinist years had been terrible and terrifying, but there is more energy in fear than in blank indifference and incomprehension. The great paradox of totalitarian regimes is that they take art and artists seriously and refuse to treat them as decorative appurtenances.

The music of Shostakovich's last decade has little of the power and vitality of his great works. It is less paradoxical, less obviously encrypted, and to some degree more emotionally open. Some of it, like the Fifteenth Quartet and his viola sonata, derives part of its power from proximity to the deathbed. Some of it, like the late romances and the Michelangelo suite, are touched by a gentleness and philosophical calm that are new to his work. And yet the great continuities remain. The organising principles of the late works are identical to those of the promising young student who presented his First Symphony as proof to his teachers that he could compose. Shostakovich's son-in-law, the film-maker Yevgeny Chukovsky, who married Galina in 1959, remembers a conversation in which Maxim asked his father why he didn't simply pay someone to copy out orchestral parts. Shostakovich replied, 'Everyone should do his own work from beginning to end.'

On 28 May 1966, Shostakovich made his last significant appearance as a pianist, playing in a concert devoted to his work that included the premiere of *Five Romances on Texts from Krokodil* (an innocuous set of songs based on the state-sponsored satirical magazine) as well as the more knowing, but not at all elegiac, *Preface to My Collected Works and a Short Reflection Upon This Preface*. Despite working with Vishnevskaya (who sang the *Krokodil* romances with Yevgeny Nesterenko), Shostakovich was crippled with nerves before the premiere. The very next night, he suffered his first heart attack.

It was perhaps a propitious time to be in convalescence. The wheel of Soviet favour and disfavour had made another creaking turn. Khrushchev had been discredited and unpersoned, and there were moves afoot to rehabilitate Stalin's reputation. In the field of literature, repression had returned. Sholokhov, with whom Shostakovich was supposed to have collaborated on *And Quiet Flows the Don*, publicly called for the death penalty for the dissident writers Yuli Daniel and Andrei Sinyavsky, who, as 'Nikolai Arzhak' and 'Abram Tertz', had criticised the regime in satirical writings published in the West. They were sentenced to seven years hard labour instead, but it became clear that with the accession of Brezhnev and a return to hard-line Stalinism, freedom of speech was effectively in abeyance. Samizdat – or clandestine – publication became the norm. Dissidence became a distinct movement. In early March 1966, the beloved poet Akhmatova died in Komarovo. She had become the most potent symbol of Russian literature through the Bolshevik Revolution and Great Terror years and, in that respect, was Shostakovich's poetic twin, but she remained to the end of her days haunted by the returning spectre of the man who had sent her son to the Gulag and made her sell her artistic soul in a fruitless bid to get him back.

Shostakovich had his own tried-and-tested method for dealing with the vagaries of politics. His String Quartet No. 11 in F minor was written at Repino in January 1966, shortly before the satirical *Preface to My Collected Works and a Short Reflection Upon This Preface*. They have the same slightly skittish quality overlying a darker vision, much like the Fool's clowning in *King Lear*. In 1964, Shostakovich told a *Pravda* interviewer that his Ninth Quartet was concerned with childhood and 'toys', but it seems that the Eleventh Quartet is closer to that playful spirit – or would be, were it not for the darker strains that throb underneath the faux-innocent surface.

The same bare simplicity surfaces in the Cello Concerto No. 2 in G major, completed while Shostakovich convalesced in the Crimea. Here, though, it is woven into an altogether more complex structure that, in the inverse ratio that applies to instrumentation and orchestration, makes the work seem sparser still. Written again for Rostropovich, it should have been conducted by Mravinsky, to whom Shostakovich still felt some loyalty. Inexplicably, or not, Mravinsky refused, claiming that he did not have enough time to learn the score. It was premiered under Yevgeny Svetlanov on Shostakovich's sixtieth birthday, 25 September 1966, on which occasion the composer was awarded the Order of Lenin and made a Hero of Socialist Labour.

Once again, Shostakovich was less excited by the medals than by the release of the film version of *Katerina Ismailova*, whose familiar motifs now seemed to haunt his work, as if his entire musical history were somehow embedded in that great work's narrative of cultural paucity, betrayal, defiance, violence, and imprisonment.

While convalescing, Shostakovich read poetry, always a solace but now an important spark to musical inspiration. Having avoided using texts for much of his career – the written word lacks the kind of ambiguity and covert protest that can be hidden away in instrumental scores – Shostakovich now seemed committed to text-setting. Forming a companion piece to the stark, almost monolinear works of 1966 is the 1967 cycle *Seven Romances on Poems by Alexander Blok* for soprano and piano trio. Its simplicity is partly explained by his physical condition. Shostakovich wrote the work for Vishnevskaya, Rostropovich, and Oistrakh, but hoped to be able to play the piano part himself. It is an intensely personal piece, beginning with a hymn to his native city and concluding with a strong assertion of the restorative power of music; Shostakovich felt that setting these resonant texts – particularly 'Ophelia's Song', another *Hamlet* reference – and working with close and sympathetic friends allowed him to overcome a deepening creative block. During the same period of recuperation, he also chose the text for what became his Fourteenth Symphony.

History still intruded, however. The new repressions introduced by the Brezhnev regime applied mainly to writers. The new weapon was psychiatry. Dissidence was officially considered a form of mental illness and treated with a variety of 'therapies' ranging from electroconvulsive shocks (replacing the bullet in the back of the head, but often almost as destructive) and large doses of insulin to simpler and older remedies such as wrapping 'patients' in freezing wet towels. Shostakovich became an important signatory to successive petitions and open letters to the authorities, pleading for a restored freedom of expression. He took up the case of Solzhenitsyn and did as the Rostropoviches had done, offering the novelist refuge at his dacha. It was a temporary alliance, because Solzhenitsyn objected to Shostakovich's militant atheism and later broke with him completely.

Nevertheless, something of the 'Jewish' solidarity of its predecessor emerges again in the Violin Concerto No. 2 in C-sharp minor, the first major orchestral work written after the 'block'. Obviously disturbed by a new wave of censorship and repression, Shostakovich sets the solo violin's plangent lament, once again owing its basic material to *Lady Macbeth of Mtsensk*, against an equally familiar two-note figure, transformed but still reminiscent of the Stalin motto of earlier works. What is different now is that 'the people' seem to have less part to play, even as an abstraction. It is as if Shostakovich now sees the essential struggle as between authority and isolated individuals like himself. It may even be that he is accusing the people themselves of a kind of self-betrayal, being too craven and hesitant to rise up and assert their freedom. The Second Violin Concerto is a complex work, troubling and magnificent by turns, majestic in parts, but constantly interrupted by a kind of violent vulgarity.

The premieres of the concerto (with Oistrakh again as soloist) and the Alexander Blok settings were played out against stirrings of dissent within the Soviet bloc. The Prague Spring was just around the corner, but, while its brutal repression sparked a passionate response from Shostakovich, for the moment he was either too case-hardened or too involved in private concerns to reflect it directly in his music. For more than thirty years, the Beethoven Quartet had been the leading chamber ensemble in Russia and had given the first performances of all his string quartets, except the first and last. Their interpretations of the late quartets only served to underline Shostakovich's growing identification with Beethoven himself, an association made explicit at the end of the viola sonata and unmissable in other works of the last years. He had been deeply troubled when, in 1965, the group's second violinist, Vasili Shirinsky, died suddenly. The 'Beethovens' had lost their original violist the year before, when Vadim Borisovsky retired, to be placed by Fyodor Druzhinin. The Eleventh Quartet was dedicated in memoriam Shirinsky, and Shostakovich then wrote his next three quartets for the other original members: the Twelfth, with its unexpected serialist elements, was written for first violinist Dmitri Tsyganov; the Thirteenth was for Borisovsky; and the Fourteenth was for Shirinsky's cellist brother, Sergei, who died during rehearsals of the Fifteenth (and final) Quartet, just months before Shostakovich's own death. It was Druzhinin who gave the premiere of the viola sonata, but only after the composer had died.

These men were as close and important to Shostakovich as Vishnevskaya, Rostropovich, and Oistrakh had become, trusted allies and friends who showed an almost telepathic understanding of the composer's needs, even if he sometimes had to give harsh criticism for misreadings (for Shostakovich, unlike the great Rubinstein, the music as written was more important than 'interpretation'). In January 1969, Oistrakh gave the first performance of the Violin Sonata, a work that, written against the bloody unravelling of the Czech experiment, rumbles with grief and anger.

That same month, Shostakovich was again in hospital. While convalescing, he began work on his Symphony No. 14. In form, it is radically different from all his other symphonies. Indeed, Shostakovich seemed to think it might not be so numbered at all, but it could not be classified as an oratorio because it was scored simply for a soprano and a bass voice with just strings and percussion. He might have wished he had excluded it from the formal list of symphonies because, as he says in *Testimony*, 'I heard more attacks on the Fourteenth than on any of my other symphonies.' According to the composer, listeners objected to the suggestion that death was the end and not some kind of beginning. Shostakovich considered how some great predecessors have approached the theme: Verdi, Tchaikovsky, Richard Strauss. But he dismissed any suggestion that death can be defied or even protested. Only Mussorgsky, as usual, seems to have got it right. To him, death always seems horrible and always premature. Shostakovich was obliged to acknowledge that there are death-like states, including the experience of waiting for execution, and chose as his text Guillaume Apollinaire's 'The Zaporozhian Cossacks'. Shostakovich was insistent at this stage in his life that the word is ultimately more trustworthy than music – so spoke a man who had tried to speak through music for most of his life and been misunderstood. The poem alluded to a moment, more famously represented in Ilya Repin's great painting *Reply of the Zaporozhian Cossacks to Sultan Mehmed IV of the Ottoman Empire*, when the Ottoman sultan, having been defeated by the Cossacks, nevertheless wrote and asked them to bend to his rule. They drafted a sarcastic reply, laden with the sultan's many titles, piling insult on him in the process and ultimately refusing his command. Repin's painting is an academic masterpiece, the delight in the faces of the men drafting the reply reflecting the people's unfailing humour in the face of oppression. Though the events in question took place in 1676, the relevance to the present moment could scarcely be missed.

Shostakovich had been inspired to write the Fourteenth Symphony by his earlier orchestration of Mussorgsky's *Songs and Dances of Death*, but the themes of mortality and the people had been sharply quickened by recent events in Czechoslovakia. The Fourteenth stands somewhat apart from the run of Shostakovich symphonies, but it is a profound and powerful experience, blackly pessimistic and almost nihilistic in its 'De profundis' section.

The authorities were well aware of its potentially subversive content and did all that they could to thwart public performance, short of an outright ban. Shostakovich was in haste to hear what he again believed might be his last, rather than latest, work, and he agreed to a private performance for invited guests in a recital room at Moscow Conservatory. He had decided to forgo using Vishnevskaya for the moment, since touring responsibilities had left her without sufficient time to learn the part. She sat in the audience, as did Solzhenitsyn, who was horrified by the work's darkness and lack of transcendence. There was a bizarre cameo during the premiere when Pavel Apostolov, Shostakovich's near-contemporary and one of his most virulent detractors in 1948, collapsed and died of a heart attack in the auditorium; Shostakovich had him for a fool, but a musically educated fool whose mission in life seemed to be to abolish music itself. Shostakovich hadn't intended to kill him, but deaths at or around musical premieres always spark superstition (think of Wagner's *Tristan und Isolde*, in which one of the lead singers died suddenly after only four performances), and it seemed like a sign. He did not feel so much rid of an old enemy as reminded once again of his own approaching death. The public premiere took place three months later in Leningrad, with Vishnevskaya and the bass Mark Reshetin. Shostakovich had enjoyed a holiday and was in considerably better spirits.

His work of the following year oscillated between public and intensely private music. He contributed a set of choruses, *Loyalty*, to mark Lenin's centenary, but also finished the film music for *King Lear*. In autumn 1970 – after yet another period in the clinic run by Gavriil Ilizarov, who pioneered the process of distraction osteogenesis and external framing of rebuilt bone – Shostakovich completed the String Quartet No. 13 in B-flat minor and the unpromising-sounding *March of the Soviet Police*. He also began making sketches for what would be his last symphony.

The beginning of 1971 must have seemed to Russians like a disturbing return to the Stalinist past. Brezhnev and his hard-line followers attempted to impose a doctrine of unlimited sovereignty over the client states of Eastern Europe, and also over Communist party members in the West and Asia. A dangerous conflict rumbled along the Sino–Soviet border. More acutely than at any time since 1962, the world seemed poised on the brink of catastrophe. Now, like in the McCarthy witch-hunts of the late 1940s and early 1950s, 'Communism' was a byword for predatory ideological imperialism.

There was a smaller and stranger return of the past in Shostakovich's life as well: a first revival of *The Nose* in Russia since 1930. Shostakovich was disinclined to concede that the work had wider and potentially political themes, somewhat contradicting his earlier insistence that the opera was a horror story rather than a joke, but its depiction of reified authority gone mad was as relevant in 1971 as it had been when first written. The long-lost score was actually found in the basement of the Bolshoi Theatre, and, despite the inevitable political shenanigans and Shostakovich's growing infirmity, he even attended some rehearsals, making the daring suggestion that a new passage (derived from Gogol) be interpolated, in which one of the characters should leave the stage and recite, 'It's amazing that anyone should write about such a subject. We've never heard the like', while pointing accusingly at Shostakovich in the audience. The *yurodivy* was still alive, if not well.

Shostakovich returned to something close to this unexpected buffoonery in his penultimate work, the *Four Verses of Captain Lebyadkin*, which he completed in January 1975. Coming so close to the end, this is a fascinating piece in which the titular character is portrayed as a rascally 'cockroach' deserving of our – not God's; such a view would never have occurred to the old atheist – forgiveness precisely because of his rascality. Shostakovich would have known that, in the complex polyphonic theatre of Dostoevsky's novel *The Possessed*, Captain Lebyadkin's sister, Marya Lebyadkin, is a classic *yurodivaia*, whose spluttering wisdom is that of a holy fool.

Shostakovich had attempted a very different (and much grander) self-association in another, somewhat earlier work, which might be accounted his last masterpiece. It is clear that in the *Suite on Verses by Michelangelo* there is a complex identification with the great artist and poet. Britten had been drawn to the subject, too, in his *Seven Sonnets of Michelangelo*, written in 1940, and he and Shostakovich may well have discussed the work at Aldeburgh in the summer of 1972. Where Britten was drawn to the putative homoerotic strain in Michelangelo, Shostakovich was attracted by more sombre themes – such as truth, love, creation, night, and death – and by similarities to the Italian poet's near-contemporary Shakespeare. There is an unmistakable echo of his *Hamlet* music in the introduction to one of the movements, which are woven together with such formidable structural – one might almost say 'sculptural' – control that 'suite' hardly seems an adequate description for this late masterpiece. The Michelangelo settings, and particularly the finale, again make use of the *yurodivy* persona, but this time, somewhat as in the Blok cycle, *sub specie aeternitatis*; this is not the Fool mocking temporal authority but Lear himself, frail and reduced, confronting the storm as Shostakovich had confronted storms throughout his life. For a non-believer, it is a position of extraordinary bravery.

Shostakovich's own physical and moral courage were never clearer than in the final three years of his life. He no longer had Stalin, Zhdanov, and Apostolov to torment him, and with the intense loyalty and support of Irina and a small circle of companions he no longer needed to fear the treachery of fair-weather friends and time-servers. In Maxim, who had settled on conducting as a profession, he had an interpreter who understood and could communicate the emotional deep structure of his work – albeit, for a further fifteen years after his father's death, under political constraints different only in degree and in rhetoric from those that had applied in 1936, 1948, and 1962.

However, the habits that develop in isolation and in permanent opposition become deeply ingrained. The late Shostakovich resembles Galileo – who had appeared in Yevtushenko's text for the final movement of the Thirteenth Symphony – in his blend of obduracy and sheer survivalism. Like the great astronomer, Shostakovich was called upon to recant, but did so murmuring his equivalent of Galileo's supposed retort, 'and yet, it moves'. What 'moved' was what always stayed the same: the endless continuity-in-change of Russia and the Russian people.

Though seriously ill, Shostakovich had completed his final orchestral work, the Symphony No. 15 in A major, in a concentrated burst of activity at Repino during July and August 1971. It is a deeply enigmatic work, on one view a simple farewell to the orchestra – almost every member of which is featured in solo – and on another a grimly satirical work, derived from Chekhovian themes, that triple-distils his disgust at Soviet society. The Brezhnev years saw a strange combination of stern centralised control and an apparent abandonment of discipline throughout society. Crime rose sharply, corruption poisoned the bureaucracy, and rates of alcoholism in the general population rose to terrifying levels. The mechanistic libertinism of the post-revolutionary years seemed to have returned, and Shostakovich captures it brilliantly in his opening movement, which is all awkward twos and threes cast in an almost cartoonish idiom. It begins with a thin chime, which seems to shake the orchestra into activity. The implication is that the people now willingly dance to the official tune, or at least march drunkenly to it.

The second movement is starkly different, mournful night-music of the most profound kind, full of sadness but also sourly dissonant. There are efforts to make the presumed protagonist conform, over-bright chords which have little to do with the surrounding music, but they fail. There is, Shostakovich seems to be saying, an unbridgeable gulf between his sensibility and that of the surrounding culture. The same impression is confirmed in the third movement, which in some respects merely unpacks and then condenses the dramatic contrast of the opening two. The finale is as densely packed with quotations, misquotations, and allusions as the rest of the symphony, and it has become a highly competitive musicological game to find them all. The most obvious is a reworking of the march from the Seventh Symphony, still recognisable but recast with disgust and resignation. The end is almost deathlike: gasps and tremors, only just governed by a fibrillating heart.

Shostakovich suffered a further heart attack during the rehearsals, which were being conducted under his supervision by Maxim. If the Fifteenth was intended as a farewell to the orchestra, that is indeed how it stands. During his last three years, Shostakovich concentrated on song-setting – including the magnificent Michelangelo suite and a sequence based on the poetry of Marina Tsvetayeva – and writing what were to be his final string quartets. It is known that he had hoped to write an eventual twenty-four quartets, a complete cycle of the keys that had been the deep structure of his musical imagination for nearly sixty years. After hearing the final pages of the Fifteenth, it is almost impossible to imagine him writing another symphony, even if health had permitted.

As it was, he completed the viola sonata between periods in hospital, working at Repino, as had been his habit. Shostakovich's health continued to worsen that summer as his cancer took hold. At the beginning of August, he suffered a prolonged choking fit that seemed to damage his heart further. Shostakovich was returned to hospital, where, six days later, he suffered respiratory failure. The agonal breathing must have sounded distressingly similar to those defeated gasps in the Fifteenth Symphony. At 7:30 in the evening of 9 August 1975, Dmitri Dmitriyevich Shostakovich died. On the same day and at approximately the same hour, thirty-three years earlier, Karl Elias had raised his baton in the sudden quiet of besieged Leningrad to begin the Seventh Symphony.

Shostakovich's civic funeral at Moscow Conservatory was a bizarre affair. Orchestral musicians were on annual leave, so there was only recorded music in the Grand Hall. Many others who might have attended were at holiday dachas in Siberia or the Crimea. In his open coffin, Shostakovich himself looked as if he too had been lying in the sun, turned unnaturally pink by the mortician's make-up. It was his last disguise, and exactly the right colour. Ministry of Culture officials and KGB men scurried about anxiously to ensure that there would be no unseemly demonstrations – not of emotion, but of dissent. Then Khrennikov rose to tell the assembled mourners what a good Communist Shostakovich had always been. Shostakovich's mortal remains were taken to Novodevichy Cemetery, where the coffin lid was sealed and the 'good Communist', free of human gaze at last, was buried to the strains of the Soviet anthem.

Six weeks later, Fyodor Druzhinin gave the first performance of the viola sonata in Leningrad. Shostakovich's complex life was over. A complex afterlife was just about to begin.

Testimony

Sometime in the latter weeks of 1974, a young music journalist called Solomon Volkov brought a typescript to Shostakovich and had him sign each chapter. Immediately afterwards, Volkov applied for an exit visa to leave the Soviet Union for the United States. He sent ahead the pages that the composer had signed, after initially lodging them in a Swiss bank. Volkov was permitted to leave in 1976 and, three years later, Harper & Row published *Testimony*, which purported to be the memoirs of Shostakovich, tape-recorded and transcribed by Volkov.

There was an immediate outcry. Not until the putative Hitler Diaries later in the decade was a text so closely examined and argued over. The Shostakovich presented in *Testimony* was a sour and vindictive renegade, viscerally hostile to the Soviet regime and scornful of fellow artists as varied as Mayakovsky, Meyerhold, Mravinsky, and Prokofiev. The 'good and loyal Communist' of the official obituaries was portrayed – or portrayed himself – as a fifth columnist who had concealed his true feelings for most of his adult life. In Russia, Volkov was vilified as a turncoat and a forger. His American publishers had scanned the pages closely for factual errors and, perhaps reassured by the composer's apparent approval, satisfied themselves that they were genuine. Even so, doubts persisted on both sides of the Iron Curtain. Those in the West who were prepared to accept that some of the book represented Shostakovich's words were inclined to believe that Volkov had embellished and enlarged the text substantially. On the Left, it was decried as a distortion, while both liberal and anti-Communist papers rushed to what seemed like a breach in the carefully defended Soviet consensus, which continued to demand absolute loyalty and orthodoxy from its artists.

There were immediate and genuine causes for concern. The composer's widow, Irina, suggested at one time that her husband had barely known Volkov, but also, at another time, that she had demanded the return of the tape transcripts – two statements that do not entirely add up. However, somewhat later, the matter seemed to be put beyond doubt when Maxim Shostakovich defected to the West and continued to insist that *Testimony* was not his father's work but an act of politically motivated ventriloquism. Only much later did he reverse his position, stating on the BBC that *Testimony* did indeed represent his father's views (which is not quite the same as confirming that they were his father's actual words). Galina, too, said that the opinions were genuine, if not the actual text.

No aspect of Shostakovich studies is more tedious or more diversionary than the controversy surrounding the authenticity of Shostakovich's 'memoir'. There is even a whisper of latent anti-Semitism in the discussion of Volkov himself, who, as a Jew, was still more-than-usually vulnerable in 1970s Russia. Some motivations in the case are easily understood. Anti-Communist observers wanted to believe that *Testimony* was the work of a great artist who had been disgracefully treated by an evil regime. Communist and 'fellow traveller' observers needed to demonstrate that the book was a travesty. Khrennikov, who had affirmed Shostakovich's political orthodoxy over his open coffin, most particularly wanted the book to be false because he was treated so harshly in it. More puzzling were the family's reactions. Irina told officials that she had asked Volkov to return the typescript at Shostakovich's behest, and that, when told it had already left the Soviet Union, she had threatened to block Volkov's exit visa. Puzzlingly, she only told this version on the eve of publication. Was she simply ensuring that the authorities believed she had taken every possible step to prevent having the great Soviet composer – a Hero of Socialist Labour and a winner of the Order of Lenin three times over – lampooned by a forger? By the same token, was Maxim's continued insistence on the book's fraudulence after his defection simply a way of protecting family members left back in the Soviet Union?

There are few straight lines and no absolute answers in the *Testimony* story. Volkov's own behaviour seems peculiar. Contrary to Irina's version, he claims to have had many meetings with Shostakovich at the artists's colony at Repino, and to have resumed these conversations when he moved to a Moscow apartment in the same building as Shostakovich. What of the claim in his preface to *Testimony* that he had tried to have the book published in the Soviet Union before Shostakovich's death? Clearly no state publisher would have touched it; its very existence would have put Volkov in considerable jeopardy. If this sequence of events were accurate, why had he sent the manuscript to Switzerland immediately after it was signed? That question at least is self-answering: it was sent abroad precisely because it was dangerous, and the only likely means of publication at home would have been samizdat, under which it would certainly have gained a reputation but also the close attention of those best placed to judge whether it was an authentic document or a farrago. International publication immediately muddied the water.

Volkov certainly knew Shostakovich. He was pictured close to Shostakovich's bier at the funeral. There is also a photograph – printed in *Testimony*, almost as a certificate of authenticity – that shows him sitting with the composer and Irina. More significantly, the photograph is signed, 'To dear Solomon Moiseyevich Volkov with affection, D. Shostakovich, 13.XI.74', an inscription that suggests a measure of intimacy between the two men and a firm date for their putative conversations. It also bears a subscription, apparently written as an afterthought: 'A reminder of our conversations about Glazunov, Zoshchenko, Meyerhold. D.S.' This tends to suggest that any references to these figures in *Testimony* – and Glazunov in particular – can be accorded some veracity. However, one can now say with reasonable certainty that, while *Testimony* almost certainly does accurately represent the real Shostakovich, at least in his later years, it equally certainly does not represent his actual words, or not in its entirety. That is, the book is true in spirit but still largely a forgery. The discovery in the text of substantial passages lifted verbatim from much earlier interviews proves that, in those cases at least, Volkov is something other than a loyal amanuensis.

What is important about *Testimony* is not so much what it said as what it sparked off. Its very existence is a catalyst for debate – MacDonald's *The New Shostakovich* is in essence an extended revisionist attempt to find the author of *Testimony* in the works themselves – but, like any true catalyst, it is unchanged by the processes it has set off and remains what it always was: a highly convincing collage and an act of brilliant and insightful projection by a passionate music lover, whose admiration and returned affection for Shostakovich was palpable. It is also important for the way it provoked open declaration of vested interest. The leftist British critic Christopher Norris sneered at *Testimony* as a hyper-subtle expression of Western wishful belief that behind those slamming social-ist-realist climaxes there had been a deeply conflicted and ironic artist who was simply putting on a show to save his life. In taking this position, though, Norris unconsciously revealed the Left's own wishful thinking: that behind those transparently ironic passages and sourly unconvincing apotheoses there was, after all, a loyal and committed Communist. One Communist Party of Britain member told the present author with absolute confidence and a show of great sadness that *Testimony* was unquestionably real, but that the opinions quoted were those of a very sick man, 'out of his mind' with pain and medication. It is a clever rationalisation, particularly given Shostakovich's failing health in 1974, but it hardly squares with the clear-sighted and technically astute composer of the Michelangelo suite or the Viola Sonata.

Decades of criticism, disappointment, poor health, and the loss of friends coloured Shostakovich's vision, but there is no reason to think of his moral agency as changed in a fundamental way by his life's experiences. Consistency may be the hobgoblin of small minds, but it can also be the defining absolute of great ones. Shostakovich made clear and sharp distinctions between what people did and who they were, preferring the former – acts, public deeds, work – to any kind of psychological or ideological explanation. That is why he was able to admire Stravinsky as an artist while excoriating him as a thinker who had turned his back on country and traditions. The fact that sometimes such opinions squared with the 'official' view does not mean that they were shaped by it or pragmatically adjusted to fit it.

In his essence – something he would not himself have believed in other than as a sum of acts – Shostakovich was not a political animal but a moralist. He had a profound but non-ideological sense of social and ethical duty, and he was genetically attached to a long Russian intellectual tradition that emphasised human improvement as a practical and philosophical absolute. Shostakovich also subscribed unquestioningly to the twin ideas of Russian exceptionalism – a conviction that Western ideas were alien to Russia's unique philosophical and cultural history – and 'Russia' as a unique and universal moral force. This was expressed in the untranslatable concept of a *dusha*, which means something close to 'spirit' or 'world-soul', and which enjoins a commitment to individual integrity, aesthetics, and practical moral awareness. Anything that did not serve those ends was by definition anti-people. Shostakovich understood good, but he equally understood evil, which is rarer, and which he would have seen in all that did not contribute to that central troika of principled ends. Experience taught him that evil cannot always be defeated by direct confrontation, but it is always susceptible to the sole qualities it is incapable of detecting: humour and irony.

The commentator Richard Taruskin made an important point about Shostakovich in an *Atlantic Monthly* review of Shostakovich's letters, as edited by Isaac Glikman. Taruskin takes to task observers like Ian MacDonald for their attempts to describe Shostakovich as a 'dissident', a term that he regards as having either no, or only anachronistic, meaning in the composer's time. To some degree, Shostakovich has been retrofitted by his biographers with all the signs of 'dissidence' – coded means of expression, deliberately contradictory positions, and apparently abrupt volte-face, sarcastic 'obedience' of the state will – but this happens with every great artist. Shakespeare, for example, has been positioned and repositioned as being royalist and republican, Catholic, gay, a proto-feminist, a commentator on race relations, and many other anachronistic positions. Part of the problem of considering Shostakovich in a similar light is that it reduces the music – and my own text is guilty of this – to a political psychodrama whose ultimate meaning cannot be discerned. In later life, Shostakovich resisted passing any substantive comment on new pieces of music, insisting that he either liked a work or he didn't, and that was that. Even this has been adduced as a sign of his weak-mindedness, when in fact it is much more likely the defensive posture of a very senior artistic figure who knows that a nod or frown from him can affect a career in a moment. Hardly anyone comments on Shostakovich's generosity of spirit or his tact.

Taruskin's way out of the issue can hardly be improved upon:

> The mature Shostakovich was not a dissident. Nor was he a modernist. The mature Shostakovich was an 'intelligent' (pronounced, Russian-style, with hard 'g'). He was heir to a noble tradition of artist and social thought – one that abhorred injustice and political repression, but also one that valued social commitment, participation in one's community and solidarity with people. Shostakovich's mature idea of art, in contrast to the egoistic traditions of Western Modernism, was based not on alienation but on service.

This is pitch-perfect. The egoism of Western modernism was as alien to Shostakovich as the idea of art for art's sake, but believing that art has a morally instructive role does not imply a belief in art as a vehicle for ideology.

The Shostakovich of *Testimony* – who is inescapably Volkov's Shostakovich, but also, in Taruskin's sense, anachronistic – is infinitely less interesting than the Shostakovich of the symphonies and the string quartets, the concertos, the chamber music, the song cycles, and the magnificent *Lady Macbeth of Mtsensk*. On the page, he can seem petty and intent on score-settling, but in his life he palpably believed that making music was a moral act and that, in a godless world, the artist brokered a relationship between power and people. Take away their programmatic titles, texts, associations, criticisms, and decrees, and his works almost invariably suggest that there are points of balance in a precarious world. He was a dialectician, to the degree that he understood dissonance to be the engine of progress, but Shostakovich fundamentally believed in harmony, and was disturbed and even horrified by his contemporaries' seeming rejection of it. His key signatures were beacons, points of light in the surrounding darkness.

That he was unable to escape history was not the tragedy in Shostakovich's life but the source of his dark comedy. Russian to his very last breath, he understood that art is never 'pure' and never entirely for itself, and yet all his life he aspired to an art that rose above politics, compromise, ideas, and fashion to become the truest expression of a lifelong commitment to his folk, a belief bravely sustained despite the distortions of National Socialism, state Communism, and the commercial trivialisation of 'folk music'.

Even if we can believe only the sentiments and not the actual text of *Testimony*, Shostakovich's credo is to be found in these words about his reorchestration of the opera *Boris Godunov*:

The people are the base of everything. The people
are here and the rulers are there. The rule forced on
the people is immoral and fundamentally inhumane.
The best intentions of individuals don't count. That's
Mussorgsky's position and I dare hope that it is also
mine. I was also caught up in Mussorgsky's certainty that
the contradictions between the rulers and the oppressed

people were insoluble, which meant that the people had to suffer cruelly without end, and become ever more embittered. The government, in its attempt to establish itself, was decaying, putrefying. Chaos and state collapse lay ahead, as prophesied by the last two scenes of the opera. I expected it to happen in 1939 … It was clear to everyone that war was coming, sooner or later it was coming. And I thought it would follow the plot of *Boris Godunov* … 'Dark darkness, impenetrable!' And 'Sorrow, sorrow for Russia, weep, oh, weep Russian people! Hungry people' cries the *yurodivy*.

Afterword

The first writing of this book now seems impossibly distant. It was always intended as a personal reaction to a body of music, rather than as an academic biography or work of musicology. Little facility in Russian – though I read it haltingly – was more of an obstacle then than it is now, and recognition that, unlike in the Cold War years of my early adulthood, travel to Russia is now relatively free and its archives suddenly open, came only rather late. Shostakovich loomed large in my childhood, and no composer except Haydn and Bartók has ever mattered quite as much. My obsession with him was even a matter of family lore. A much-loved cousin of my father's – David died young of a medieval ailment that turned a gentle man into an unrecognisable monster – once came to our house in Paisley. I was installed, as family photographs confirm, in an outsize armchair beside the radiogram, 'reading' an upside-down copy of *Reader's Digest*. Cousin David settled into a chair and awaited the offered cup of tea.

'This is impressive stuff,' he said, indicating the radio and the glowing Third Programme dial. 'Is it Mahler?'

This apparently enraged me.

'No! It Shockastokevich.'

Collapse of adults; beginnings of an unwelcome reputation for cultural precocity.

So Shostakovich came to me early and never went away, even after I learned to pronounce the name correctly. I must have heard it mentioned often enough to garble it, but I first consciously heard of him when my father recounted listening to the Seventh Symphony broadcast from Leningrad during the siege, picked up on short-wave radio in a West Lothian colliery house. That moment alone made Shostakovich seem urgent and essential. When later I learned of his life and travails, he increasingly came to seem not just the last great exponent of the European symphonic tradition, but a figure who represented most of the contradictions facing a twentieth-century artist.

In fact, my father's devotion to Shostakovich only extended to the Seventh and backwards to the problematic Fifth, which has always been the sticking point in even the most modest foray into Shostakovich studies. The idea of an artist saying sorry is almost anathema to us. To adapt a famous movie tag line: being an artist means *never* having to say you're sorry. And yet Shostakovich had apparently been put in that position. Even early on, after a morbid immersion in all the classic literature of totalitarianism – with its 'disappeared', its unpersons, its industrial numbers of dead and imprisoned – the thing that struck me most about Shostakovich, and seemed the key to his attraction and mystery, was precisely that he survived when so many others had not.

I am not a musicologist. My music education was limited to yawn-punctuated class singing and, later, listening to the

Brandenburg Concertos while our music teacher attempted to augur the winner of the 2:30 at Uttoxeter. I have always vaguely associated J.S. Bach with the *Sporting Life*. In the same way, I associate Shostakovich with the smell of hot valves, overcooked food, and my parents' throat-tickling Richmond Tipped. Like school, home was inconsistent in its musical encouragement. Mother would not have an instrument in the house; while my father was musical and played piano by ear, he was bound by the same rule of silence. His large collection of 78s and early LPs was rarely accessed when we were all together, though I learned to play the records quietly when *The Black and White Minstrel Show* was on downstairs, with the TV – an exception to the rule of loudness – cranked up high enough for the residents of Numbers 29 and 33 to share in the questionable fun. That Oscar Lampe's solo in Richard Strauss's *Ein Heldenleben* would have to be my first *Desert Island Discs* choice bespeaks a fairly odd kind of childhood; it moved in parallel to more zeitgeisty sounds.

Like those who learn German in order to read Heine or Goethe, I learned about music in order to understand Shostakovich, while learning in parallel that a knowledge of sonata form, the cycle of fifths, and the notional 'mood' of different key signatures was only the beginning of the story. This book is not a personal account of Shostakovich in the usual sense. I had no desire in 2006 to write something like Nicholson Baker's *U and I*, which traces his personal and literary involvement with John Updike, nor to write an *In Search of...* study in which the author's adventures in the archive and among his subject's family and friends are the main part of the story.

I did attempt to learn Russian in order to read about Shostakovich, but it was futile because until well after 1991 everything that was written in Russian about Shostakovich had to be taken not with a pinch but with a whole salt mine.

So, the text that precedes this afterword was not intended to be authoritative or definitive, nor unduly subjective, either, but rather a plain account of the most extraordinary and heart-rending artistic story of the modern age. In many respects, Shostakovich is only awkwardly representative of his era in music. In purely stylistic terms he can seem an outlier, resistant to the dominant twelve-tone language of the mid-century, and while he later made use of tone rows in a number of mature works, he never surrendered to the philosophy wholesale.

It will be clear, and my book perhaps only reinforces the injustice, that Shostakovich's music is still only discussed in terms of his presumed ideological leanings and a veritable mise en abyme of ironies, evasions, and disguises. This is perhaps not the best way to listen to him at all, and the only advice I can offer – despite any contrary impression in the preceding pages – is to listen to him for the music, not for an unrecoverable narrative. The fifteen symphonies mark the last act in a classical tradition that had perhaps already played out in Western Europe and the United States, hence a certain old-fashioned quality to Shostakovich's writing. The string quartets more comfortably fit a modernist conception of chamber music as a confessional form, deeply private but at least notionally self-revealing. The concertante works were more than usually personalised, written either for Shostakovich himself or for close friends and family. There were, in addition, other canonical works like the late viola sonata, which marks a definite cadence to the career and a poignant summing up of its major concerns. His beloved opera *Lady Macbeth of Mtsensk* attracts more admiration than devotion outside Russia, its sensibilities so much in keeping with a strain of literature that remains difficult for non-Russians to decode. It pulsates with unmistakable life and energy – though, following a dramatic and very public volte-face by Stalin, it came close to ending Shostakovich's public career before it had properly begun. Almost everything that followed was received and analysed in light of the composer's standing with and attitude toward the regime, a process retrofitted to cover work that came before 'Muddle Instead of Music'. Most problematic was a vast body of occasional music written for theatre, film, and ballet and regarded with suspicion because commissioned by the state or officially sanctioned. The prevailing narrative demands that this work be treated as minor and inconsequential, the result of compromise and mauvaise foi, and yet even the most casual audition suggests that the theatre music contains some of Shostakovich's most vivid and exciting music, not at all the work of the left hand.

It is a confusing picture, then. Stripped of its contexts, the work would still be immense, but those contexts are so dramatic and overdetermining that a purely musicological approach to Shostakovich proves difficult, even at this distance from the events and the ideological to-ings and fro-ings that so profoundly affected his career. Shostakovich himself more than once insisted that he listened to (others') music simply *as* music – but this may be the evasion of a senior composer who does not want to show favouritism by issuing imprimaturs, or it may be the natural instinct of a man whose own work was repeatedly subject to loyalty tests and the party line.

And yet, for most new listeners, the backstory will seem as remote as the machinations of eighteenth-century European courts, which doubtless played a part in the emergence of the classical canon. One wonders what a listener exposed to the Fifth Symphony, or the Seventh and Eighth, would make of the music, when offered no guideline as to the composer's identity, nationality, and thought. Personal experience – my children, students, the odd friend who has expressed inter-est in what I am listening to – suggests that newcomers find Shostakovich quite overwhelming, which seems to me an excellent starting place.

Any backstory aside, his is one of a very few bodies of art that invariably stiffens moral resolve. This is not because his work offers any clear moral message beyond an innate com-mitment to democracy (that much is audible even without programme notes), but because of Shostakovich's commit-ment to work – and *work*, rather than *the* work. That in itself makes him old-fashioned and unmodern, a throwback to an earlier concept of artist-as-craftsman. Shostakovich's meticu-lousness, far from being a neurotic tic, was the ticking heart of his method.

Of his courage, there can be no doubt; of his wisdom, occasionally. The path of defection and exile always, presum-ably, lay open to him, but – even leaving aside the fear that he would be punished by proxy, with the whole left-behind family sent to the Gulag – Shostakovich knew that he could not function in the West and that Russia was his well and his wellness. Whether any Westerner can fully understand him remains an open question, even now that the Russian archive has opened and access to those living who knew him has eased. Even from that limited perspective, his greatness seems to me total, even more generously so than when I first wrote. We are used to hyphenating life and work as if they were, ideally, the same thing. Perhaps Dmitri Shostakovich breaks that connection, proving that the rough places and exigencies of life, the pressures of society, and the dead weight of ideology need not stand in the way of art.

Acknowledgements

Gestures of authorial thanks can be awkwardly self-flattering and not much more dignified than glowing drop-quotes on the paperback cover. Writing is essentially a lonely business; even though the writer stands on the shoulders of giants, he sometimes declines to link arms with the living. However, I had early help – even if they weren't aware of it – from Gerard McBurney, the doyen of Shostakovich studies in Britain; the late Ian MacDonald; and Rhodri Jeffreys-Jones of the University of Edinburgh, whom I first met as an undergraduate. Colleagues in the music department at BBC Scotland also offered valuable insights, so thanks to Hugh MacDonald, David McGuinness, and Svend Brown.

The largest debt is owed to my late father, Robert Stanley Morton – who revered two Shostakovich symphonies but seemed oddly indifferent to the rest – and to my family: my wife, Sarah; daughters, Fiona and Alice; son, John; and grandson, Jack (who is the responsibility of Fiona, and to whom this edition is dedicated).